Overcoming Life's Toughest Problems

Ed Hindson

HARVEST HOUSE PUBLISHERS
Eugene, Oregon 97402

Cover by Alan Furst Design, Minneapolis, Minnesota

OVERCOMING LIFE'S TOUGHEST PROBLEMS

Copyright © 1999 Ed Hindson
Published by Harvest House Publishers
Eugene, Oregon 97402

Library of Congress Cataloging-in-Publication Data

Hindson, Edward E.
    Overcoming life's toughest problems / Ed Hindson.
        p. cm.
    ISBN 0-7369-0009-8
    1. Suffering—Religious aspects—Christianity.
    2. Christian life—Baptist authors.   I. Title.
    BV909.H55 1999   98-31334
    248.8'6—DC21   CIP

99 00 01 02 03 04 05 / BC / 10 9 8 7 6 5 4 3 2 1

To

Dr. Jay Adams
and
Dr. Howard Eyrich

For their friendship, counsel, and
confidence in the grace of God.

CONTENTS

—⚭—

An Invitation to
Renewed Hope

—ɷ—

Roads are meant to be traveled, but sometimes they can get pretty rough. Life is such a road. It can lead to excitement and adventure or it can lead to failure and despair. Life is never all joy and no sadness. It is never success without failure or gain without pain. No matter who travels life's paths there will be obstacles to face and pitfalls to avoid.

This book is written to encourage fellow travelers on the rough road of life. The longer you travel life's highway the more you will realize that life is a journey of faith. Martin Luther once said, "We are not yet what we shall be but we are growing toward it; the process is not yet finished but it is going on; this is not the end but it is the road."

No matter how much personal preparation you have made for the journey there will be obstacles ahead about which you never dreamed. Problems will have to be faced and decisions will have to be made. In every crisis of life there will be lessons to be learned and new growth to be attained. In every difficult circumstance you will be faced with the realities of life itself. At each new juncture you will have to decide the direction your life will take. At times there will be others to help you along. But sometimes you will find yourself traveling all alone. Do not despair, for when you need Him most God is there. He will share your heartaches, bear your burdens, and help you find the answers to your problems.

God has spoken to us in the inspired pages of His Word. There we find divine guidance for the problems of life. And it is there that we receive the assurance of His grace to see us through. No matter what you may be facing, God is there to help you.

This book is about finding the answers to the problems of life. It is also about finding God's grace to sustain us in the process. It is a book of hope that points us back to the Bible as the greatest source book of all time. By principle or precept, the Bible speaks to every major problem of life and assures us of God's hope and help.

I want to thank my dear friend and former student, Dr. Tim Clinton, president of the American Association of Christian Counselors (AACC), for his personal encouragement in this project, and Mrs. Emily Boothe, who typed the original manuscript and provided several helpful suggestions. I pray that God will use the advice given in these chapters to help those who are seeking His grace for the journey of life.

—Dr. Ed Hindson
There's Hope!
Atlanta, Georgia

CHAPTER ONE

HOW TO HANDLE LIFE'S TOUGHEST PROBLEMS

—⟋⟋—

E verybody has problems! We can't get very far on the road of life without encountering them. Sooner or later we all face challenges and difficulties which push us to the limits of our ability to cope. The nature and complexity of those problems may differ, but to the one struggling with them, they are very real.

I have spent a lifetime helping people work through their problems, and I am continually amazed at what I learn from those who are experiencing God's grace in the process of their struggles. There are no simple solutions or easy answers to life's toughest problems. God reminds us that He is the only One who has the answers for hurting hearts, broken lives, and searching souls.

The message of the Bible is one of help for the hurting. In its pages are the greatest resources in all the world. These timeless truths have stood the test of endurance generation after generation. Instead of new theories and experimental attempts, the Bible offers solid advice based upon the inspired truths of the

Word of God. These truths tell us that God alone can and will help us deal with our problems.

While we experience the blessings of God in our daily lives, life is not without its difficulties, challenges, and struggles. The Bible reminds us that God comforts us *in* our troubles, not necessarily *from* our troubles (2 Corinthians 1:4). In fact, suffering and trouble are His methods of shaping our lives and our character. In some cases, God may use the worst of circumstances to accomplish the best of results for our own good.

> *The very fact that you are going through a difficult time may be the greatest indication that God is at work in your life.*

The Bible reminds us that God is greater than our problems. Since He rules the universe, He can overrule every circumstance of life for our own good. Romans 8:28 reminds us, "We know that in all things God works for the good of those who love him, who have been called according to his purpose."

In our human weakness, we want to run from problems, while God wants to use those problems for our own good. The very fact that you are going through a difficult time may be the greatest indication that God is at work in your life. Rarely do we learn the deep lessons of life when everything is going well.

The real learning comes when everything goes wrong! That's when God usually gets our attention. When the bottom falls out of our life and there is nowhere else to turn, we will find ourselves instinctively calling on God for help. There is something basic to human nature that drives us to God when we come to the end of ourselves. Even unbelievers will cry, "God help me!" when faced with a crisis.

Taking the First Step

How we handle our problems is the key to overcoming them. Our reaction will determine whether our problems become opportunities for personal growth or the means of spiritual and emotional defeat. Learning how to handle life's problems with the *right heart attitude* is the first step in overcoming them.

Wrong attitudes express our inner frustration with life and our bitterness toward God for allowing problems to come into our lives in the first place. They are symptoms of our refusal to believe that God is really in control of our lives. Ultimately, wrong attitudes push us away from God instead of drawing us to Him.

Running from God is like running away from the one person who can really help you. The more you run, the more He will pursue you like the "hound of heaven." His grace will keep reaching out to you even when you don't want it. Hebrews 6:19 reminds us that Jesus Christ is our "hope as an anchor for the soul, firm and secure." This passage goes on to explain that He has anchored us to the heart of God, beyond the veil into the Holy of Holies in heaven itself. You may have run far enough to pull the links of the chain to their limit, but God will not let you go if you belong to Him.

The tug in your heart is the pull on the chain of the anchor of hope. That restless dissatisfaction in your soul is the stirring of the Spirit to draw you back to the God who loves you. Your unwillingness to let go of Him is the evidence of His grace in your life. He has not given up on you. In fact, He may have just begun His greatest work in you.

We begin conquering our problems when we face them. As long as we deny that we have a problem, we will never really deal with it. Whether we realize it or not, most of our problems are the result of our own sinful responses to life's challenges. Only when we face that sin and admit it will we take responsibility to correct it. The Bible calls this process confession and repentance (Luke 13:3; 1 John 1:9).

The basic procedure for dealing with most of life's problems is relatively simple:

1. *Face reality.* Stop pretending things are fine when they are not. Denial will keep you from dealing with your problems. It may make you feel better for a while, but it

will not solve your problems. The sooner you face reality, the better your chances of recovery.

2. **Take responsibility.** Be willing to take action to deal with your own problems. No one else can solve your problems for you. They can encourage, help, and support you in your crisis, but ultimately only you can take the responsible steps of action to correct your own problems.

3. **Do right.** There is a right way and a wrong way to handle every problem. Find the right way and do it! God's Word will guide you. It specifically tells us how to handle life's toughest problems.

Trusting God to Help Us

Much of the New Testament deals with crises. Several letters (epistles) were written specifically to deal with problems like divorce, lawsuits, sickness, death, divisions, heresies, immorality, disorder, and marriage and family problems. There is hardly a problem today that Christians face that is not covered in the pages of Scripture. If we really want to know God's will for our lives in dealing with a particular problem, the Bible will guide us to the answer. Consider, for example, the following account:

"I thought I was doing the right thing," Tom said. "We needed the money and I didn't intend to keep working at that pace forever. Before I knew it, Julie took the kids and moved in with one of her friends."

> *The key to handling our problems is learning to trust what God tells us to do about them.*

Tom went on to explain that he had been working out of town six days a week for nearly two years. Sometimes he was gone for as much as three weeks at a time. Julie felt neglected and unloved. Her pleas to him seemed to go unanswered, so one day she left and took the children with her.

"What can I do to get her back?" Tom asked. "I never meant for it to end like this!"

Tom and Julie's story is not unusual. In fact, it is all too often a reality for today's couples struggling with the pressures of modern life. Decisions about marriage, work, and family are often made with little regard for biblical teaching on these matters, which is so essential for effective and successful living.

The key to handling our problems is learning to trust what God tells us to do about them. Too many people want to make their own decisions and then ask God to "bless" what they have already decided. Instead, we need to figure out what God wants us to do and do it with the confidence that He will bless it. Our obedience to His commands places us in a position to receive His blessings in our lives.

Our willingness to trust God in every circumstance of life depends on our confidence in His love. All uncertainty on our part is an expression of distrust in His love. It is a basic rejection of God's character and nature. When we fail to trust Him with our problems we are really distrusting His sincerity and integrity. Because He truly is an all-loving God with our best interests in mind, we must learn to trust His love for us in spite of our circumstances.

Finding His Purpose in It All

Tom and Julie's marital crisis caused a temporary separation, but it also got their attention focused in the right direction. They stopped pretending everything was all right and finally did something about it. It wasn't easy, but they started doing what they should have been doing all along—honestly talking about their feelings, praying together, and seeking the kind of biblical counseling that could help them put things back together. In time, they were able to deal with their problems head-on and solve them.

Whether we fully understand it or not, God is sovereign over the events in our lives. Jay Adams says, "No matter how bad the crisis may appear to be, it is never beyond His ability to resolve it."[1] Every crisis in our lives is part of God's sovereign purpose for us. We may not understand that purpose while we are going through the struggle, but we will eventually see how the circumstance was for our benefit.

Effective biblical counseling must introduce God as the most basic, vital, and hopeful person in our lives. He alone is fully equipped to meet our needs, shape our lives, and get us through our problems. Dr. Adams writes, "The counselor's task is to relate God fully to the crisis. It is crucial for Him to restructure the entire picture as one in which God is at work achieving His purposes. . . . To do this so profoundly changes the crisis that it takes on an entirely new dimension. It becomes a crisis in which *God is involved.*"[2]

This basic truth, so often overlooked in Christian self-help popular psychology books, is fundamental to any proper understanding of life's problems from a distinctively Christian viewpoint. If God is really present, then we are not alone in dealing with our problems. If His sovereign will prevails over those problems, then there are three things of which we can be certain:

1. *God's sovereignty limits our crisis.*

   God is in control of our lives and He limits the extent and duration of the crisis. God limited Satan's attack in the case of Job (1:12; 2:6). Jesus warned Peter that Satan would "sift" him as wheat but assured Peter that He had prayed for his restoration (Luke 22:31-32). The Bible makes it clear that nothing can touch us that is beyond the limits of God's sovereign control.

2. *God's sovereignty brings meaning to our problems.*

   The problems of life are not tragic episodes in the absurd saga of human existence. There is purpose and meaning to our struggles, problems, and sorrows. Romans 8:18 promises "that our present sufferings are not worth comparing with the glory that will be revealed in us." Jay Adams says of our struggle, "There is something worthwhile, something exciting, something adventurous, something holy in it . . . because there is a point to it all: God is in the crisis!"[3]

3. *God's sovereignty assures us of His grace.*

There is no problem in life that is beyond the grace of God. He will help us in our time of need. When the apostle Paul struggled with his "thorn in the flesh," God assured him, "My grace is sufficient for you, for my power is made perfect in weakness" (2 Corinthians 12:9). The Bible also tells us, "Cast all your anxiety on him because he cares for you" (1 Peter 5:7). God's grace is sufficient for every problem we face.

Making the Commitment

The biblical concept of faith is that of a deep personal commitment that leads to a step of action on our part. The Bible never defines faith as mere intellectual assent. Nowhere in Scripture do we find people merely giving God an affirming nod. Real faith involves a total commitment of one's self to God.

When a person is genuinely converted, he or she believes the promise of God to the point of surrendering their lives to Him. We may not understand every nuance of that commitment, but we know that we have believed the gospel to the point that it has resulted in a life-changing commitment to Jesus Christ.

That same kind of commitment is necessary in trusting God to help us with our problems. I have always been amazed that people will trust God to forgive their sin, give them eternal life and a home in heaven, but they will not trust Him to help them with their problems here and now!

Halfhearted commitments will not help you solve your problems. Either God can help you or He can't. Either you trust Him or you don't. It is that simple. Most of us try to complicate matters by assuming the solutions to our problems have to be more complex. But Jesus simply said, "Come to me, all you who are weary and burdened, and I will give you rest. Take my yoke upon you and learn from me, for I am gentle and humble in heart, and you will find rest for your souls" (Matthew 11:28-29).

Jesus is our role model for spiritual and mental health. While most of us are "weary and burdened," He is "gentle and humble."

In the face of His own crucifixion, the Bible tells us, "he did not retaliate . . . he made no threats." What did He do? "He entrusted himself to him who judges justly" (1 Peter 2:23). That means that Jesus Himself had to completely trust God the Father to turn the injustice of the cross into something that could serve the sovereign purpose of God.

> *Faith is not a blind leap into the dark. Faith is believing the principles of God's Word and ordering our life accordingly.*

If Jesus had to learn to trust God, how much more do we? Every crisis in our lives is an opportunity for us to grow in grace, but we usually respond in such a way that the crisis drives us further from God's grace. Instead of becoming more like Christ, we often become less like Him. That is why Gary Collins has said, "The emphasis on discipleship is so central to the teaching of the New Testament and so basic to the Christian way of life that it would be impossible to ignore it whenever the Christian enters a counseling or other helping relationship."[4]

The key to handling our problems is learning to trust God with them. If we don't do that, we won't solve our problems. And if we won't commit our problems to God, we won't grow in His grace. We will remain stuck in our own self-absorbed indecision and inability to solve our problems.

The *process of trust* can be simply diagrammed like this:

"It can't be that simple!" Tom insisted. "If that was all there was to it, I would do it."

"Would you?" I asked deliberately.

"Yeah. Sure I would," he responded.

"Then let me put it this way," I suggested. "If your job is ruining your marriage, will you trust God enough to give up your job if it is necessary to save your marriage?"

"That's a lot to ask," Tom said hesitantly.

"No," I replied, "that's faith!"

Faith is not a blind leap into the dark. Faith is believing the principles of God's Word and ordering our lives accordingly. God tells us how to live successfully. He doesn't leave us in the dark regarding His will for our lives. He spells it out for us in the Bible. The bottom line is: Either we trust God or we don't.

The ultimate question is: *Do you trust God or don't you?* The answer to that question will determine how you handle life's toughest problems. You can do it your way . . . or you can do it His way.

Which way will you choose?

CHAPTER TWO

FACING A CRISIS
WITH CONFIDENCE

—∭—

A crisis is anything that breaks the normal pattern of life. It is generally an unusual situation that disrupts your normal life. It may lead to either growth or disaster. Also, it will often bring about a major turning point in your life for good or bad. You can't control the crises that come into your life, but you can control your reactions to those crises.

Dealing with a crisis will usually make you face something in your life that you would rather not deal with. It will often force us to grow spiritually and emotionally in an area that we would never choose for ourselves. Therefore, even the worst of problems can be used by God to produce the best possible results in our lives.

The major impact of a crisis is that it disrupts the normal balance in our lives. Each of us is involved in a personal "balancing act" in our daily lives. We juggle spiritual, physical, and emotional responses to life's challenges every single day. Even on the best of days, there are little glitches with which we must cope. These rarely lead to a crisis because we are used to dealing with these minor challenges. A crisis occurs when we face a major challenge and our ability to juggle responsibilities falls apart.

You can't control the crises that come into your life, but you can control your reactions to those crises.

Crises come in several ways. Not all crises are alike. But each type of crisis disrupts our lives in such a way it challenges us to find better ways of dealing with our problems. *Types of crises* are generally listed in five categories:

1. *Situational.* These occur when situations beyond our control affect our lives. These include sickness, accidents, and personal conflicts. The situation itself dictates the nature of the crisis (e.g., car accident).

2. *Dispositional.* These are crises that are triggered by our emotional responses. They include anger, bitterness, worry, fear, and hostility. In these crises our own feelings trigger the nature of the crisis (e.g., an argument that leads to an angry outburst that is an expression of pent-up frustration).

3. *Life-transitional.* Sometimes a crisis can occur simply because we are going through a transition that we find difficult to cope with at the moment. These can include things like moving, changing jobs, a new career, retirement, or old age. Each of these involves making mental and emotional adjustments to a new phase of life that may seem overwhelming at first.

4. *Developmental.* These are maturational crises that often come as we develop from one stage of life to another. Going from childhood to adolescence to adulthood has always been a challenge. Some people handle it better than others. For some, these become the major crises of their lives.

5. *Traumatic.* Crises brought on by traumatic events like rape, robbery, crime, death, murder, legal action, or even an impending divorce can shatter a person's emotional stability and plunge him or her into a psychological breakdown. Victimization of children, women, the elderly, or those with life-threatening diseases is all too common.

The Stages of a Crisis

Every crisis is unique to itself, but there are some general stages to crises which typically follow a similar pattern. Jayne Crisp adapts the three stages recognized by Morton Bard and Dawn Sangrey as a typical pattern:[1]

1. *First Stage: Impact*

   How to Help: Achieve Contact. The first characteristic of a crisis is that it strikes without warning and threatens one's safety and security. Crisp writes: "The *impact* or initial stage of the crisis often leaves people feeling numb, shocked, dazed, out of control, and in a state of disbelief and vulnerability."[2] Often at this point, the safety and security needs of the person in crisis are primary. The initial contact may involve calming and assuring the person in order to settle him or her down.

2. *Second Stage: Recoil*

   How to Help: Clarify the Problem. During this stage, the person in crisis may experience confusion and emotional isolation. This may last for days or months. Crisp suggests: "Boil down the problem by allowing individuals to talk about the event in an effort to 'normalize' the trauma and reduce the profound sense of isolation the person may experience."[3]

3. *Third Stage: Reorganization*

   How to Help: Cultivate Coping Skills. How a person handles the crisis will often determine whether he or she learns from the experience. During this stage people tend to reassess their goals and plans. They may even reevaluate their whole life. This is the point where positive spiritual decisions can lead to life-changing opportunities. The shattering experience of a divorce, death of a loved one, or loss of a job can often become the turning point in a person's life.

The Pattern of a Crisis

Both secular and Christian counselors generally recognize that crises follow a fairly typical profile. When a person experiences the shock of a crisis, he or she is usually thrown out of balance by it. Donna Aguilera and Janice Messick refer to this pattern as going from a state of equilibrium (balance) to one of dis-equilibrium (imbalance).[4] They suggest the following diagram of a crisis:

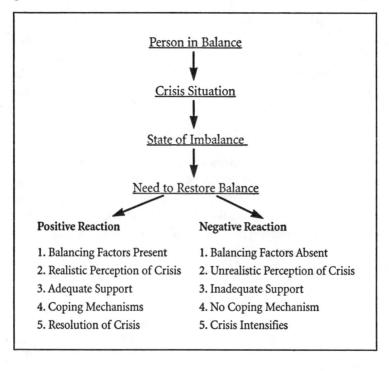

Person in Balance

Crisis Situation

State of Imbalance

Need to Restore Balance

Positive Reaction	Negative Reaction
1. Balancing Factors Present	1. Balancing Factors Absent
2. Realistic Perception of Crisis	2. Unrealistic Perception of Crisis
3. Adequate Support	3. Inadequate Support
4. Coping Mechanisms	4. No Coping Mechanism
5. Resolution of Crisis	5. Crisis Intensifies

It is important to notice that a crisis is usually short-lived. At the moment of the initial impact of the crisis it is not necessary to resolve all of one's basic life issues, problems, and struggles. The most important thing we can do is to help someone regain their spiritual, mental, and emotional balance at that point. Later, other issues can be addressed. For example, if a man's wife has just left him and he is threatening to kill himself, it is more important to deal with the threat of suicide before you try to resolve any of the issues in the marriage.

In most crisis situations the person in crisis goes through the following *phases of crisis:*

1. *Rise in Tension.* As the pressures build, the individual becomes more and more stressed by the factors contributing to the crisis.
2. *Inability to Cope.* Eventually the person in crisis reaches a "breaking point" where he or she just can't take it anymore.
3. *Emergency.* The psychological breaking point usually precipitates a crisis emergency, when things get completely out of hand and beyond one's control.
4. *Disorganization.* The crisis results when a person cannot handle the emergencies of life. A state of major disorganization results, leaving the person unable to cope with the crisis.

When a person loses his or her job, such a crisis often results. The rise in tension occurs as a person anticipates losing the job. An inability to cope may force the individual into a state of panic, isolation, or denial. After the job loss, it is not uncommon for the individual to sit at home aimlessly waiting for someone to offer him or her another job. A pattern of irresponsibility may result, which keeps the person in a constant state of inactivity.

Possible Responses to a Crisis

People in a state of crisis often lose control of their lives. They become out of touch with their own feelings and react in a variety of ways they might ordinarily never choose under normal circumstances. These responses may include:

1. *Shock.* Some people go into a state of psychological shock as a defense mechanism toward the deep impact of the crisis. It is not unusual for the victim of an automobile accident to wander around afterward muttering about a small scratch on his shoes when his car has just been totaled.

2. *Anxiety.* A state of perpetual anxiety often follows the initial shock of the crisis. Accident victims will often experience nightmares about their accident. Fears and phobias about traveling may result for some time to follow.

3. *Depression.* The trauma of shock and anxiety tend to wear a person out emotionally, leaving him or her in a state of depression. This may last for a few days, months, or even years. Such depression usually doesn't leave the individual until he or she feels "safe" again.

4. *Violence.* Suppressed anger and fear often explode to the surface in outbursts of anger, hostility, and violence. A mother who has just lost her husband may become unusually angry with her son because he didn't help her with the dishes or clean up his room. She is focusing her anger on a minor issue that is a safer "target" than, say, being mad at God for taking her husband.

5. *False-adaptation.* One of the most difficult responses to detect is that of a *pseudo* (false) response. These occur when a person acts happy in spite of a lost job or a spouse's death—yet in reality, the person is not happy. Such a response is little more than wishful thinking "packaged" as spiritually and psychologically correct attitudes.

When we do not learn to respond biblically to our crises, we will inevitably blow up one way or another. This is especially "tempting" if we think we aren't supposed to cry, express anger, or get upset. "Masking" over our emotions only suppresses them in a way in which they might still affect us in the future.

Considering the Limitations

Every crisis situation poses certain limitations by the very nature of the crisis itself. When we attempt to minister to those in crisis, we must remember these limitations:

1. *Time is brief.* The nature of a crisis is generally short-lived. Therefore, we don't have a lot of time to decide what to do. Whether we are dealing with our own situation or trying to help someone else, we will have to act quickly. This is not the time for a long, drawn-out process.

2. *Focus on the immediate issues.* What is causing the crisis, and what can you do about it? Get to the heart of the matter—don't beat around the bush. There may be several peripheral issues that relate to the crisis but aren't as urgent as the central issue(s). Deal with those later. Focus your immediate attention on the most serious issue(s) involved in eliminating the crisis.

3. *Emphasize present behavior.* In a crisis there is little time to evaluate psychological patterns, past behavior, and spiritual progress. Crisis intervention must focus on present behavior. Christian crisis counseling must further focus on discerning proper biblical responses. The person experiencing the crisis needs to ask, "What does God want me to do right now in light of this particular crisis?"

4. *Establish short-term goals.* You can't fix everything during a crisis, but you can deal effectively with the most important issues at hand. After a couple has had a fight and one

of them has left, it will be necessary to get them together and get them talking again before they are ready to ask forgiveness and recommit to each other.

Setting the Goals

The basic goals in dealing with a crisis should shape our approach to our own crises and our ministry to others in crisis. Secular models generally encourage these steps:

1. Resolve the immediate crisis
2. Encourage personal growth
3. Increase coping mechanisms

All three of these are valid and suitable goals for anyone seeking to help people in a crisis. Christians, however, will recognize there is a great deal more to this picture than secular counselors generally recognize.

> *You* can face any crisis with confidence when you remember that God is in control of the crisis.

First, the resolution of the immediate crisis must follow clear biblical prescriptions. If a couple were to separate over a series of arguments, secular counselors might recommend a prolonged separation or "cooling off" period. Biblical guidelines, however, are different: First Corinthians 7:10-11 tells married couples not to separate. Then it adds that if they do separate, they should follow these principles: 1) remain unmarried; 2) be reconciled; 3) don't divorce. From this one passage we can safely offer this advise to those in troubled marriages:

1. Don't separate unless it is absolutely necessary
2. Don't start dating or looking for another partner
3. Work hard at reconciliation
4. Don't see divorce as an option

Second, "personal growth" must be defined as spiritual growth. People use the word *growth* loosely today. Biblically, growth indicates a spiritual maturity as our lives are conformed to the image of Christ (Romans 8:29; 12:1-2).

Third, "coping mechanisms" are more than self-help tips, group reinforcement, or collective emotional expressions. Biblical coping mechanisms include:

1. Personal relationship with Jesus Christ
2. Intimate communication with God
3. Prayer and Bible study
4. Christian counseling
5. Christian discipline
6. Church fellowship
7. Empowerment of the Holy Spirit

When all of these elements are in place in a believer's life, there will be more than adequate coping going on—there will be genuine spiritual growth. A crisis doesn't have to defeat you. God can help you learn valuable lessons from it that will make you a better person in the long run. Don't give up because you're facing a tough time; the crisis you are in right now may be the most important learning opportunity and growth advantage you have ever experienced.

You can face any crisis with confidence when you remember that God is in control of the crisis. He is greater than your problems and His grace is sufficient to meet your needs. He won't let you slip beyond the grasp of His grace. Romans 8:37-39 reminds us, "No, in all these things we are more than conquerors through him who loved us. For I am convinced that [nothing] . . . will be able to separate us from the love of God that is in Christ Jesus our Lord."

CHAPTER THREE

UNDERSTANDING YOUR EMOTIONS

—⟋⟍—

E motions are the feelings that fuel our reactions to life's challenges. They can make us soar to the heights of happiness or plunge us into the depths of despair. Sometimes our emotions burst out and surprise us—like crying at a wedding, laughing at a funeral, or getting angry at a best friend.

We can't always control the initial outburst of emotion, but we can learn to deal with it. If we don't, we may end up letting our emotions destroy our lives, our family, and our friends.

Anger can be a very destructive emotion. It can make a person say or do things he or she will regret for a lifetime. Anger can dent a friendship, damage a relationship, or destroy a marriage. Out of control, anger can become the most destructive force in the world. Yet, under proper control and coming from a righteous motive, it can be a powerfully positive force for good.

The Greek word for anger is *orge*, meaning "any natural impulse." Anger is among the strongest of all passions. But the Bible makes it clear that not all anger is necessarily sinful. In fact, Scripture states that "God . . . expresses his wrath every day"

(Psalm 7:11). There is much in the Bible about the anger and wrath of God toward sin. God hates sin, but He does not hate it sinfully. Expressions of anger at sinful acts are normal and sometimes even necessary.

> *Angry responses usually do not solve problems. They make them worse!*

The apostle Paul admonishes us to be angry and sin not (Ephesians 4:26). This injunction clearly shows it is possible to feel righteous indignation over some heinous act of sin. Every decent person becomes angry over the mass murder of innocent people, for example. Nevertheless, it is difficult to limit our anger to righteous indignation. We usually become more indignant than righteous!

That is why Paul goes on in Ephesians 4 to warn us not to let the sun go down upon our wrath lest we give the devil a place to work in our lives (verses 26-27). When we become angry and stay angry, we can ultimately end up hurting ourselves worse than the original offense did.

Anger gets out of control when we fail to deal with it properly. It can lead to all sorts of conflicts and offenses. Jesus Himself warned us, "It is impossible but that offences will come" (Luke 17:1 KJV). Being a Christian does not give you a spiritual insurance policy against hurt; what you need to learn is how to handle it.

Dealing with Anger

Angry responses usually do not solve problems. They make them worse! When we blow up or clam up because of anger, we are really saying, "Go away. I don't want to deal with you." Thus, sinful anger prevents genuine communication. It builds barriers instead of bridges. Simple ventilation (blowing up) lets everyone know you are angry and will chase them away. On the other hand, internalization (clamming up) does not really hide your anger and will cause people to avoid you because they sense something is wrong.

There are at least five steps a person can take to deal successfully with an anger-producing situation:

Step 1: Rethink the situation. James tells us, "Everyone should be quick to listen, slow to speak and slow to become angry" (James 1:19). Proverbs 25:8 likewise warns us not to embroil ourselves hastily with our neighbor. When you feel anger welling up in your heart, ask yourself, "Have I really been wronged, or am I overreacting?" Evaluate the situation. Remember—appearances can be misleading!

Step 2: Reestablish God's value system. The Bible teaches very clearly that God has a system for establishing the worth of people based on love and acceptance, whereas the world has a system for establishing the worth of people based on competitive hostility. From 1 Corinthians chapter 13 we can draw a clear comparison of these two value systems:

How God Values People	How the World Treats People
1. *Love is patient.* God is understanding of human nature and not only forgives the mistakes of men with great patience, but does not push or rush individuals into changes that are not in their best interest.	1. *Anger has no patience with people.* Anger demands its own way, immediately, and is willing to sacrifice the best interest of other people in pursuit of its own goals. True patience is unknown to the angry person.
2. *Love is kind.* Whereas patience involves the lack of a nasty reaction to another person, kindness is a positive reaction of reaching out to assist or help another person. It is a positive regard for the needs of others.	2. *Anger is cruel.* Not only is anger impatient, but anger sees weakness in another person as an opportunity to take advantage of that person. The angry individual sees kindness as an unnecessary weakness.
3. *Love does not envy.* Love does not see another person's success as a threat, and is not uneasy over accolades to another person. The loving person sees his worth as secure in the Lord, and is not jeopardized by the achievements of others. Love genuinely wishes the best for others.	3. *Anger thrives on envy.* The angry person believes that others' success is always to some degree at the expense of his own self-advancement. Therefore he is threatened by the achievements of others, often envious of their accomplishments, and seeks to overtake them by any means possible. He is willing to undermine others in pursuing his own success.

4. *Love does not boast and is not proud.* Love does not believe that it deserves better than it has, and is careful not to be proud of its own achievements at the expense of others. The loving person is truly humble and sincerely cares about others.

4. *Anger has a proud walk.* The angry person sees pride as a weapon with which to intimidate others. Although God has much to say against pride, the angry person uses boasting and the "pride of life" as a ready means to validate his own worth and seek an advantage over others.

5. *Love is not rude.* Love always takes into account the sensitivities of other people. Love understands the temperaments, emotional makeup, and background that make each person unique, deserving of respect and courtesy at all times.

5. *Anger is pushy and often discourteous.* The angry person sees common courtesies and the sensitivities of others as bothersome distractions in his headlong course of self-aggrandizement. The angry person has no real desire to put other people at ease or show genuine concern for their well-being.

6. *Love is not self-seeking.* Love's first purpose in life is not to assure its own success, pleasure, or security. Love honestly and genuinely seeks the good of others. This kind of behavior comes only from the heart of one in whom the Holy Spirit dwells and has active control.

6. *Anger always seeks its own good first.* The angry person sees life as a slugfest whose motto is "To the victor belongs the spoils." To the angry person, winning and getting ahead is not everything, it is the *only* thing. Anger feeds the self-centered ambition.

7. *Love is not easily provoked.* Love is patient when it comes to reacting to others emotionally. Love has a flexible and understanding approach to others. It appreciates the need for restraint and calmness in the great majority of life's situations. Cutting words, petty comments, and divisive rumors are not the by-products of a loving heart.

7. *Anger is easily provoked by the actions of others.* Anger views impulsive action as both an acceptable and effective means to gain its own ends. "Hair-trigger temper" describes the ease with which an angry person can be provoked. The angry person erupts easily and often.

8. *Love does not bear grudges.* Love understands that forgiveness is the controlling force through which God and man are able to have a relationship. Love understands that no relationship can flourish without forgiveness, and certainly there can be no depth in communication.	8. *Anger always remembers an offense.* Bearing grudges, harboring resentment, and taking revenge characterize the chronically angry person's response to the problems and setbacks of life. Not only does anger not overlook a wrong suffered, but rather it engraves a record of the offense on the stone of its heart for permanent remembrance.
9. *Love does not rejoice when it sees people making mistakes.* Love hopes the best for people and is heartbroken when they choose to disobey God. Love never gloats when those who flout God's Word suffer the consequences. Loving people are forgiving people.	9. *Anger takes pleasure in the calamity of others.* Anger perceives that those who violate God's Word and therefore experience personal tragedy are "getting what they deserve." While preserving a pious exterior, the angry person secretly hopes others will fall as far away from the Lord as he or she is.

Step 3: Repent of any unwillingness to forgive. We are to value the people who have wronged us as being worthy of love and acceptance. The Scriptures teach plainly that to enjoy God's continued forgiveness and blessings ourselves, we must be willing to forgive others the wrongs they have done us. In Matthew 6:14-15, Christ states emphatically that God will not allow us to reestablish good fellowship with Him until we have forgiven others and made up our differences with them. God further states that He will not honor the prayers of those who maintain an unwillingness to forgive others for wrongdoings. If God reckons another person worthy of His love and acceptance, any contempt on our part must be repented of in order to learn to forgive.

Scripture states in Philippians 2:6-7 that Christ set an example for us by valuing Himself no higher than the Father. He was willing to set aside His divine prerogatives while retaining His divine nature. The first aspect of His emptying was this relinquishing of His "rights and privileges" of deity to live as a man. However, a second important aspect of this emptying was His role-modeling to mankind of how to empty oneself of unfruitful emotions. We must be willing to repent of any disdain or contempt for others. A person who has truly emptied himself of all feelings of self-pity, injustice, disgust, and pride in relation to others has captured the secret of overcoming anger.

Step 4: Redirect your energy toward a solution. Once we have dealt with an episode of anger through the steps just outlined, we will likely sense a tremendous amount of emotional energy still present. These "aftershocks" are the debris that remains after we have spiritually and rationally changed our mind about the anger-producing situation. This emotional energy can cause discomfort and tension—if it is not constructively channeled. The redirection of our anger involves turning our original anger into constructive, solution-oriented planning to alleviate the problem. Productivity, not hostility, is the path to personal growth and maturity.

Step 5: Rely on trusted, spiritually mature Christians for counseling. Scripture teaches that a faithful friend can provide valuable insights—both spiritual and practical—during times of difficulty. Proverbs 12:15 says that the foolish person always sees things through his own eyes, but the wise person asks for sound counsel. There are also times when the confession of a wrongful act or an insensitive attitude to a brother or sister in Christ can be a spiritually strengthening and deepening experience. James 5:16 suggests the value of such confession—both in deepening spiritual unity and in hastening the solution to difficult problems. Encouraging one another is also an important part of this fifth step. Hebrews 3:13 says we are to encourage one another day after day as quickly as possible. Why is encouragement important? Because it preserves us from spiritual hardness. It keeps us from thinking that we are alone and unsupported in our struggle.

The Alternative to Anger

"Do not let the sun go down while you are still angry" (Ephesians 4:26). The longer you stay angry, the more hardened you will become toward the person who hurt you. When we rebel at the circumstances of life, we are really rebelling against

God, since He controls those circumstances. Such an attitude says, *I could run the world much better!* The angry man, like the worrier, is attempting the impossible: He is trying to do God's job for Him.

Every Christian is indwelt by the Holy Spirit (Romans 8:9) and has the potential to produce the fruit of the Spirit: love, joy, peace, patience, gentleness, goodness, faith, meekness, and self-control (Galatians 5:22-23). Ultimately, there is no excuse for harboring sinful anger because God has made every provision for conquering it with loving forgiveness. The Bible's alternative to anger is to "put it away" and replace it with kindness, tenderness, and forgiveness (Ephesians 4:31-32).

In the steps listed earlier, I have tried to give a series of steps that are helpful for dealing with the problem of anger. Only active resistance can keep the Spirit from producing His fruit in our life. Thus, the angry Christian must face the fact that he is in rebellion against God.

Anger can lead to more sinful attitudes and actions, such as hatred, malice, revenge, blasphemy, and even murder. Like a lighted fuse on a bomb, anger can trigger a multitude of explosive responses. Hatred is a bitter enmity called *echthra* in Greek. It is the opposite of *agape* (divine love). Malice (from the Latin *malus*, or "evil") means a wrongful desire to destroy or harm someone. Revenge (Greek, *ekdikeo*) means to hurt someone in return for their hurting you. *Blasphemy* actually is a Greek word brought over into the English language, meaning to "speak evil" of someone. Murder (Greek, *phoneuo*) begins with anger in the heart (Matthew 5:21-22).

This progression of evil begins with bitterness and spreads like a plague. Anger is the outward expression of an inward bitterness. Hatred that is left uncontrolled can even lead to murder. Such hatred is the opposite of genuine love, which forgives and forgets the offenses of others.

Remember, God did not stay angry against us. He loved us in spite of our sin and sent His Son to die for that sin. In so doing, He offered us forgiveness and everlasting life. His is a total and immediate forgiveness. No wonder we who have been so thoroughly forgiven are told to be "forgiving each other, just as in Christ God forgave you" (Ephesians 4:32).

"You really hurt me," Sandra told Jack. "I want to forgive you, but I'm not sure I can."

"Why not?" Jack asked nervously.

"I'm not sure I'm over hating you!" she replied.

> *R*emember, God did not stay angry against us. He loved us in spite of our sin.

Sandra's attitude is typical of those who have been hurt. Our typical response to hurt is anger. But as Christians we also realize we can't stay angry.

Rebuke and Forgiveness

Pain is one of those emotional hurts that we can't avoid. But it doesn't have to turn us bitter or destroy us. Bitterness is the most dangerous of all attitudes to healthy living. It will eat away the vitality of your spiritual life until your once-vibrant testimony is in shambles. It is the cancer of the soul, claiming millions of victims every year. It spreads faster than the common cold and threatens the survival of many churches. But we are not left without hope; there is a dynamic cure for this dreadful scourge.

The principle of forgiveness is a truly powerful force in the believer's life. It can melt the hardest heart and clear the most clouded conscience. When used properly, forgiveness paves the way for reconciliation between the worst of enemies. It is often the key to the abundant blessings of God as it unlocks the soul to the work of the Holy Spirit.

Life is full of hurts, and it always will be! As long as you live, people are going to offend you, hurt you, and disappoint you. But you needn't let their actions control your response and outlook on life. You can learn to rise above life's disappointments.

Jesus told His disciples to handle the problem of offenses and bitterness by learning to forgive. We must do likewise. Jesus said, "If your brother sins, rebuke him, and if he repents, forgive him" (Luke 17:3). Notice that we have two obligations when we are offended: The first is to *rebuke*, and the second is to *forgive*.

A rebuke is not blowing up at someone. Rather, it is a plain statement of truth: "What you said really bothered me." "It hurt me to know you felt that way." Remember, it takes spiritual maturity to give a rebuke in the right spirit, and to receive rebuke that way, too! The Bible teaches we are to speak "the truth in love" (Ephesians 4:15).

Learning Lessons from Life

Everyday life is often our best teacher. Some of the greatest lessons we can ever learn are from well-intended rebukes we receive from others—especially our friends. However, in order to learn those lessons, we cannot allow ourselves to view a rebuke with hostility.

Jesus put it this way: "Why do you look at the speck of sawdust in your brother's eye and pay no attention to the plank in your own eye?" (Luke 6:41). All too often we fail to realize how badly we are behaving. That is why the believer is to rebuke those who offend him rather than spreading the offense through gossip. We are to go directly to the person who is the source of the offense (Matthew 18:15). Failure to do so may result in the most serious of consequences—God withholding His forgiveness of our own sins! (Matthew 18:33,35).

Unity and oneness among Christians is a serious matter with God. He considers a longstanding grudge against another person a major setback in the Christian's life. Christ states in John 17:17-21 that *sanctity* (the Christlikeness of the believer) is largely measurable by the *oneness* (unity) that exists between that believer and others.

Considering the importance to God of such oneness among Christians, it would be good to examine the proper way to accept a rebuke from another believer without becoming offended. In the chart on the next page, we can see how taking offense at another person usually generates one of four different feelings.

We tend to feel either disgruntled (angry), disappointed (hurt), deceived (used), or defensive (accused).

Each of these four feelings is based on an underlying idea we have in our minds. In the case of the *disgruntled* (angry) person, the underlying idea is, "I've been offended." In the case of the *disappointed* person, the underlying idea is, "I've been betrayed; someone has let me down." The person who feels *deceived* says, "I've been manipulated, even used." The *defensive* person's response is, "I've been potentially threatened or accused without grounds."

THE FEELING BEING GENERATED	THE UNDERLYING IDEA
I feel disgruntled (angry).	I've been mistreated (abused).
I feel disappointed (hurt).	I've been betrayed (let down).
I feel deceived.	I've been manipulated (used).
I feel defensive.	I've been threatened (accused).

Our Lord told His disciples that if someone offended them seven times a day and repented each time, they should forgive him—to which the apostles said to the Lord, "Increase our faith!" (Luke 17:5). Jesus then told them that if they had "faith as small as a mustard seed" (Luke 17:6), they could move trees. In other words, "You don't need more faith—use the little you already have." The more we exercise our faith, the greater it becomes.

Seeing Ourselves as God Sees Us

In order to further help His disciples understand the importance of the powerful principle of forgiveness, Jesus shared the parable of the unprofitable servants (Luke 17:7-10). In this story, Christ dealt with the disciples' attitudes toward themselves and others. He reminded them that ultimately, they were "unprofitable." He wanted them to see themselves as they really were. Selfish and insecure people get angry and are easily offended. They often try to compensate for this by trying to make people think they are more important than anyone else. They can never figure out why the world does not revolve around them and their plans. Therefore, they suppose that God doesn't really care for them. They become easily upset when things do not go their way. They never see themselves as God actually sees them. In order to learn to forgive others effectively, they must ultimately see themselves for what they really are—unprofitable servants, yet immensely and unconditionally loved by God. Only then are they (and we) in a proper position for God to work in our lives.

Excuses for Not Forgiving

Out of selfishness, we will often muster a variety of excuses for not forgiving. These include:

- Revenge (*I enjoy hating him.*)
- Anger (*I'm too upset to forgive.*)
- Jealousy (*I can't let him do this.*)
- Fear (*I'll be hurt again.*)
- Pride (*I was right; he was wrong.*)
- Emotion (*I don't feel like forgiving.*)
- Self-righteousness (*He doesn't deserve it.*)
- Guilt (*I can't even forgive myself.*)
- Suffering (*I'm just too hurt to forgive.*)
- Worry (*What if he doesn't understand?*)

The ultimate excuse is "I can't forgive," which really means "I won't forgive!" You may not *feel* like forgiving, but that doesn't exempt you from God's command to forgive willingly. You can do anything that is right; God always empowers us to do what is right. His grace is always sufficient, no matter how difficult the task. When we forgive others, we confirm what Christ did for us on the cross when He died for our sins so that we might be forgiven.

Let the Power of God Loose in Your Life!

Scripture clearly states that wrong attitudes grieve the Holy Spirit and hamper God's work in our lives: "Get rid of all bitterness, rage and anger, brawling and slander, along with every form of malice. Be kind and compassionate to one another, forgiving each other, just as in Christ God forgave you" (Ephesians 4:31-32).

We must put away all wrong feelings that stem from bitterness. The chain reaction of bitterness can easily lead to open conflict that hurts others and damages the cause of Christ. We must learn to forgive others just as completely and totally as God has forgiven us.

The powerful, positive principle of forgiveness will unlock our embittered spirit and set the power of God free in our soul. It will make us kind, tenderhearted, and forgiving. It will make us like Christ.

Understanding Our Feelings

Feelings are a normal part of everyday life. At a football game, we get excited; at a funeral, we are usually sad; at a family reunion, we are filled with joy. Feelings affect, and often control, the greater part of our lives. They represent our perception of our physical and emotional condition. Thus we often say, "I *feel* great!" or, "I *feel* lousy." We even stretch the word *feeling* to include attitudes, judgments, and convictions. "How do you feel about our foreign policy?" someone asks. The answer to such a question will not be a statement of one's feelings, but rather one's beliefs.

We live in a feeling-oriented society. "If it feels good, do it!" is the existential motto of our age. Everyone seems to be giving in to his feelings and setting aside his convictions. Traditional beliefs yield to the narcissistic pursuit of self-gratification. Feelings are everything—a principle that has betrayed many a Christian into outright sin. Excuses are legion: "But I feel so much better when I'm with her." "Can't I do this and still love God?" "Doesn't God want us to be happy?" When we ask such questions, what we are really questioning is God's standards for our lives.

Feelings Are Symptoms

Our emotions tell us what is really going on inside us. They are often by-products of our thinking. If, for example, we think a human being dies at death, then the death of a loved one will leave us prostrate. If we think that we are ugly or inferior, we will *feel* ugly or inferior. Inferiority in itself is not a feeling; it is a value judgment we make about ourselves. Guilt, likewise, is a feeling—one that comes from behavior. If you do something you think is wrong, you will feel guilty.

Some people do not *feel* saved. That should not surprise us, since the conviction that one is saved is not an emotion. Assurance is not a feeling, but a belief. Distinguishing between our feelings and our beliefs and behavior is essential to solving our problems.

Our attitudes reflect our true inner beliefs about ourselves and our problems. "I can't!" really means "I won't!" Anxiety, hatred, envy, grief, fear—all reflect how we think. Non-biblical thinking will always result in non-biblical actions. For example, non-biblical thinking tells you that you have a right to do whatever you want, and if someone tries to stop you, you will retaliate. Biblical revelation, however, tells you not to strike back (1 Timothy 3:3) and to turn the other cheek (Matthew 5:39).

Feelings Can Be Dangerous

Our feelings are the symptoms of our true inner thinking. They are changeable when our thoughts and beliefs change. Feelings are guides that can help us better understand what's occurring within us, but they are not good guides for establishing a permanent course of action. To impulsively follow our feelings rather than God's Word is the worst thing we can do. To deny our feelings and resolve to do what is right is not hypocrisy, but character. We may not realize it, but there are times when we will go against our feelings—such as getting up out of bed when we'd rather stay in.

If we allow our feelings to dictate our actions, we can easily end up doing that which is irresponsible, such as skipping school, lying to someone, or running away from a situation. We may feel like doing these things, but that doesn't make them right. Christian morality (behavior) is clearly outlined in the Word of God. The Bible itself is the final authority for our lives—not our feelings.

Overcoming Our Feelings

Self-discipline comes only when we learn the art of self-denial. We are in a lifelong struggle against our feelings. In order to live the Spirit-controlled life we must die to ourselves. Scripture admonishes, "Offer your bodies as living sacrifices, holy and pleasing to God. . . . Do not conform any longer to the pattern of this world, but be transformed by the renewing of your mind" (Romans 12:1-2). We have to learn to *think* like Christians in order to *behave* like Christians. We need to think biblically in order to behave biblically. Right thinking and right behavior will then result in right feelings. You will feel right when you know you have done right.

We need to be careful not to let our feelings rule the various aspects of our lives. While it's important for us to understand how we really feel and why we feel that way, we can never let our feelings become the final standard of right and wrong. One woman may feel good about her abortion while another feels guilty. A husband may feel his divorce is of God, while his wife feels that it is of the devil! Who is right? Are all feelings relative to each person's own experience and perception? If they are, then the statements and commands of Scripture are meaningless and can be quickly dismissed by those who feel they do not apply to them.

The ultimate standard by which we must judge our feelings is the Word of God. No matter how we feel, God's Word gives us an unbiased declaration of His truth. Remember, Jesus said, "You will know the truth, and the truth will set you free" (John 8:32). God's truth liberates us from our feelings. Truth sets our soul free for fellowship with God. It is His Word of truth that sanctifies us and equips us for life and service. No matter how we feel, one truth stands paramount above all others—God loves us!

CHAPTER FOUR

DEALING WITH DEPRESSION

—〰—

J ulie angrily threw her hairbrush at the mirror, causing the mirror to chip. "What are you doing?" Brad asked anxiously.

"I just can't take it anymore!" Julie sobbed. "I hate my hair, I hate myself, and I hate being alive!"

Brad hadn't realized the way Julie was feeling; this outburst was the first indication that she was depressed. However, this became only the first episode in a long series of similar outbursts.

Most people experience depression at some point in their lives. It's a far more common problem than many people realize. It is a form of self-imposed isolation that may be spiritually, emotionally, or physically caused. Physical illness, the loss of a loved one, the sense that one has failed, and many other difficulties may lead a person to become depressed.

Even great men of God became depressed for significant periods of their lives: Job, Moses, and Elijah all wished at some point that they would die. David became deeply depressed over his sin, and Jeremiah grieved greatly for the sins of the people of Israel.

A depressed person may suffer more real pain than a person with a physical illness. One of the most distressing things about depression is the realization that there is often no simple solution for it. Certain physical conditions (such as a chemical imbalance, menopausal change, or hypoglycemia) may cause depression as a side-effect. On the other hand, it is equally dangerous to minimize the symptoms of depression. Pretending that nothing is bothering you will *not* cause your depression to go away.

The Cause of Depression

Physical Causes

Depression is sometimes caused by physical conditions that are unrelated to spiritual problems. Any disruption of the physical processes of the brain can lead to chemical imbalances within the nervous system, causing depression. The brain relies on several key chemical substances that help a person to maintain a stable mood. An imbalance of any of these chemical substances can lead to drastic mood swings and depression.

Other physical causes of depression include hypoglycemia (low blood sugar); hypothyroidism; endocrine hormone imbalances in blood levels of estrogen or adrenalin; viral infections such as the flu or mononucleosis; vitamin shortages; drug misuse; exposure to industrial poisons; fatigue; and premenstrual syndrome (PMS). These physical problems cannot be overcome merely by tending to one's spiritual condition. Rather, they must be diagnosed and treated by a qualified physician or psychiatrist.

Most depression, however, has a spiritual and psychological cause rather than a physical one. Depression is most serious among the divorced, the widowed, the unemployed, the guilty, the lonely, the empty. Loss of meaningfulness to one's self and to others often causes serious depression. Lack of self-worth, lack of feeling essential to others, and a lack of intimacy with God may all contribute to one's becoming depressed. Because God is the "God of all comfort" (2 Corinthians 1:3), He is the only source of victory over spiritual depression. Whether we want to admit it or not, non-biological depression is a spiritual problem, and calls for a spiritual solution.

Spiritual Causes

Following is the unhappy sequence of events that unfolds in the development of depression brought on by a spiritual crisis of unconfessed and persistent sin in the life of a believer:

Sin

The breaking of fellowship between God and man is the most devastating aspect of sin. Sin is a choice contrary to God's biblical commands in pursuit of our own wants. The outcome of a willful refusal to obey God is that we will reap painful consequences (Hosea 8:7).

Anxiety

The Scriptures teach that sin not only causes a separation between God and man (Psalms 66:18), but sin causes anxiety in the heart of the believer: "I am full of anxiety because of my sin" (Psalm 38:18 NASB).

Confession and restoration of our relationship with the Lord can be one choice we make when we find ourselves under the anxiety caused by sin. "He who conceals his sins does not prosper, but whoever confesses and renounces them finds mercy" (Proverbs 28:13).

Depression

Denial of the sin at hand, and a refusal to confess it and make it right with God, now tumbles the Christian into real depression. Psalm 39:2 says that when we keep silent about our sin, the sorrow grows worse.

Despair

Once depression is a continual part of our existence, then the sadness of the heart can lead to brokenness (despair) of the very will to live. The Bible says, "When the heart is sad, the spirit is broken" (Proverbs 15:13 NASB).

Breakdown

The final state of this process is a breakdown of the fabric of the personality, referred to in Scripture as a "drying up of the bones," and sometimes popularly called a nervous breakdown. "A man's spirit sustains him in sickness, but a crushed spirit who can bear?" (Proverbs 18:14).

Depression may be fueled by circumstances far beyond our control, but depression is often the end result of not handling our problems scripturally. For example, the Bible reminds us, "Do not be anxious about anything, but in everything, by prayer and petition, with thanksgiving, present your requests to God. And the peace of God, which transcends all understanding, will guard your hearts and your minds in Christ Jesus" (Philippians 4:6-7).

This passage makes it clear that worry and anxiety come from a lack of prayer. It is common for believers to insist that they have prayed about their problems, but the counseling process often reveals that they have not really communicated with God at all. Rather, they have simply muttered their frustrations to God, which is not the same as praying! God makes Himself accessible to us for guidance because He wants us to take action against the problems and discouragement of life. However, we need to offer up our concerns to Him in genuine prayer, willingly yielding those concerns to His control and submitting our hearts and minds to His direction.

The Side Effects of Depression

Inner Conflict That Leads to External Results

The spiritual conflict that underlies a person's depression will always come to the surface with definite physical and emotional consequences:

- Hopelessness
- Fear of the future
- Worry
- Pessimism
- Irritability
- Inability to concentrate
- Fear of dying
- Fear of change
- Lack of confidence
- Constant headaches
- Loss of sex drive
- Withdrawal from people

In essence, depression is a form of self-pity. It is a self-inflicted means of escape from responsibility in the real world. Something about that person's world is not quite right (from his or her human perspective), and that bothers that individual. Eventually discouragement can give way to depression. What initially bothers that person could be anything: health, family, job conditions, inadequate future security, fear of growing older, and so forth.

It is not *what* is bothering the person that is so important, but *how* he or she is handling it. Whenever we become discouraged, defeated, or embittered by our circumstances, we are really questioning God's sovereign control over those circumstances. *How can He really be in control,* we think to ourselves, *and let this happen?* Our self-centered view of the problem only pushes us further into depression.

Self-Centeredness That Leads to Self-Destruction

The major cause of suicide is depression. Once a person views the world from a self-centered perspective and concludes that things just are not going to go his way, he may want to escape from that world. As a result, one person commits suicide every 20 minutes in the United States alone! There are seven suicides listed in the Bible (Abimelech, Samson, Saul, Saul's armor-bearer,

Ahithophel, Zimri, and Judas Iscariot), and all of them were the result of sinful actions.

Sometimes people commit emotional suicide instead of physical suicide. They cut off all their emotional feelings toward God and people. They withdraw into their own inner closet and shut the door of their life. This can lead to what psychiatrists call a *psychotic depression,* where the person altogether loses touch with reality. God wants us to open the door and get out of the closet! God wants us emotionally healthy!

> *Even depression can ultimately produce good results in our life if we will allow God to use it properly.*

Depression does not need to defeat us or destroy us. It can actually become God's tool to discipline us into correcting wrong thinking and wrong behavior in our life. According to Romans 8:28, "all things ... work together for good to those who love God, to those who are the called according to His purpose." Even depression can ultimately produce good results in our life if we will allow God to use it properly.

God made us with the *capacity* for depression; however, He did not intend it to defeat us, but to correct us. If we sinfully resist God's purpose in our lives, we are especially vulnerable to serious depression. "But I can't help it," you say. "I don't want to feel this way." You may not want to suffer the consequences of depression, but you will not be able to overcome depression by simply wanting, wishing, or praying it away. You will need to move out in faith along a road of positive action.

Overcoming Depression

Depression often leads to hopelessness. When you are depressed, you feel disinclined to do anything about it (usually because you are not really sure what to do). Yet, you *must take action!*

1. *Believe that God is greater than your problems.* Whatever circumstances have you down, it is not the end of the world. Look up—God can help you.

2. *Turn all those problems over to Him in prayer.* Do not just say words—*communicate* with God (take time with Him). Pray specifically, listing each area of concern. Don't just pray that God will take your problems away, but pray that He will give you an understanding of each problem and a mental strategy of how to attack each problem one step at a time. Follow this daily with a plan of action and a prayer for the courage to take just one step forward in faith against each problem each day.

3. *Believe in God's purpose despite your difficult circumstances.* What is He trying to accomplish in your life through these circumstances? How are you resisting Him? Seek out a wise pastor, trained counselor, or mature friend for an objective opinion on your situation and how you are responding to it (Proverbs 11:14).

4. *Recognize that depression feeds on self-pity, which must be confessed and forsaken as sin.* Do not just patch things up on the surface. Deal with your deeper problem of a poor self-image. Squarely face your self-centered attitude and confess it as sin. The opposite of depression is joy. Scripture reminds us, "The joy of the LORD is your strength" (Nehemiah 8:10). When joy is missing, your strength is gone!

5. *Realize that you cannot always have your own way.* Submission to life's circumstances is really submission to God's will for your life. Frustration and anxiety never solve anything. Remember the truth of 1 Corinthians 10:13: "No temptation has seized you except what is common to man. And God is faithful; he will not let you be tempted beyond what you can bear. But when you are tempted, he will also provide a way out so that you can stand up under it."

6. *Acknowledge you have no valid excuse for staying depressed.* Determine to do everything necessary to conquer your depression! Stop pampering yourself, and start living for others. God will not put more *on* you than He will put *in* you to help you handle it.

7. Get up, get out—face reality. God is alive and at work in your life. Remember, sinful thinking *(God doesn't love me; He can't help me)* is just as harmful as sinful behavior. Not only do wrong actions produce wrong feelings, but wrong thinking also produces wrong feelings. Remember, you are a child of God. Act like it!

8. Avoid major stress. Some of the tension-producing stresses in life can be minimized. Avoid too many major changes all at once. For example, buying a home, changing careers, and having a baby all in one year may place a lot of stress on a person.

A change of pace in what we do from day to day can also help relieve the minor stresses of life. Too much of any activity—whether study, work, or housekeeping—can get you down. Take a genuine break, do something you enjoy, go somewhere different. There's always a way to make time to treat yourself to something you truly enjoy.

9. Get some exercise. Being "good and tired" from vigorous physical exercise helps you relax, helps you sleep, improves your appearance, and gives you the satisfaction of feeling physically fit. It's best to make exercise a regular part of your daily routine, and recent medical research indicates that regular exercise may actually result in biochemical changes within the brain that help to offset depression.

10. Confess and forsake sinful actions and sinful thinking. Think scripturally, like a real Christian—then act like one. Stop making excuses and start making some changes.

11. Get your priorities in proper order. Put God first, not yourself. Stop trying to make everything revolve around you and your problems. From a truly Christian perspective, you have no real problems. Instead, you have lots of opportunities to trust your heavenly Father and see Him work in your life.

12. Get involved with the needs of somebody else. Get your eyes off yourself and onto the needs of others. You cease being a missionary when you become a mission field. Remember, Jesus Christ has already commissioned you to go to others. *Christ*-centered thinking is not morbidly self-centered thinking. Positive Christian thinking is God-conscious, not problem-conscious.

Remember, the opposite of depression is joy. The Bible tells us that joy is a fruit of the Spirit (Galatians 5:22). Therefore, the solution to non-physically caused depression is spiritual in nature. The depressed person has become the victim of his or her feelings. When we feel slighted or neglected depression sets in. Remember, God is greater than our feelings. He is the source of real joy. We need to let Him fill the void and restore the joy of our salvation. "A cheerful heart is good medicine . . . " (Proverbs 17:22).

Dealing with Guilt

We cannot fully overcome depression until we have dealt sufficiently with guilt. Guilt comes from a troubled conscience. It is a self-judgment based on perceived personal misconduct. It may or may not deepen into sorrow or remorse. Some people, in fact, sublimate their guilt. The Bible tells us their consciences are seared (1 Timothy 4:2), and they seldom show regret for what they do.

All sin initially produces guilt in the soul of the sinner. When guilt weighs heavy on our sinful soul, it drives us to God for forgiveness. If, however, we fail to obtain that forgiveness, or if we persist in our sin, we may deaden (sear) our consciences and become insensitive to guilt. Nevertheless, we are still guilty before God. A murderer may feel no remorse for his crime but he will still pay the penalty just the same. Whether we sin ignorantly or willfully, we stand condemned before the law (Romans 2:12).

The Psychological Effects of Guilt

No one is a stranger to guilt. However, we all deal with it differently.

Guilt is a major factor in psychological problems. Often we respond to guilt with *defense mechanisms*—denial, blame-shifting, suppression, sublimation, self-justification, and so forth. All these, in fact, are means that people use instinctively to deal with guilt on a psychological level. Guilt feelings stimulate self-condemnation in the form of anxiety, inferiority, fear, worry, and pessimism. When these are not resolved, they lead to psychological camouflage, to diversionary behaviors such as withdrawing from others or drug abuse, and eventually to depression.

All guilt is real guilt. A person is guilty, by biblical definition, when he has broken God's moral law (Romans 3:19). Also by biblical definition, a person's sins (and his real guilt) are washed away when confession occurs (1 John 1:9). However, guilt *feelings* are another matter. A person may be guilty of sin and yet not feel guilty. Another person may feel guilty over something that is not sinful. Guilt feelings based on a personal sense of chronic inferiority before God are sometimes referred to as "false guilt." These guilt feelings are real enough, but it's the standard by which we judge ourselves as inferior that is false. The standard may indeed not be legitimate (dreams of unattainable perfection, for instance), but our violation of that standard will still produce a real sense of guilt. The solution to this kind of guilt is to acknowledge and correct our false standards, not merely explain away our guilty feelings.

For example, a person may grow up being told that it is sinful to wear red socks. If he believes that standard to be true but chooses to violate it, he will experience guilt. The solution is not for this person to deny the reality of his guilt, but for him to reexamine his standard. Once he is convinced the standard is invalid, the guilt will disappear.

The Moral Conflict

It is in the area of dealing with guilt that Christian theology and secular psychology have their greatest conflict. If there is no God and, therefore, no divine standard of behavior, there is no true guilt. All guilt would then be "false guilt" arising from a faulty value system. Guilt would merely be the result of violating generally accepted cultural norms rather than universal principles. If we lived in a culture where murder, cannibalism, rape, adultery, incest, and stealing were acceptable behavior, then people would feel no real guilt over committing those acts—at least, that's what some say.

Christians, however, will have none of that! We believe that real guilt arises from sinful actions that can only be truly forgiven by God. Criminals often admit to feeling guilt over crimes that they thought were justifiable.

The Types of Guilt

Objective Guilt

Objective guilt is personal guilt resulting from the violation of an objective standard: legal, social, personal, or divine. Violating civil law, social law, or our own personal standards results in real guilt, as does the violation of God's laws. In order to face the issue of objective guilt, we must acknowledge the legitimacy of the standard that condemns us. True guilt is intended by God to drive us to repentance and change. And, with God's help, correction and restoration are possible.

Subjective Guilt

Subjective guilt is the sense of regret, shame, or condemnation we experience when we believe we have done wrong. These guilt feelings may cause us to face our sin and deal with it. However, some of us will come to feel guilty out of proportion to our act of sin. Subjective guilt is a fallible and sometimes irrational judgment we pass on ourselves. It is self-condemnation, generating feelings of worthlessness and depression. Subjective guilt varies with our feelings about ourselves and the way we act. It is based on a fallible measure rather than an objective standard.

Resolving Guilt

Two principles stand clear in Scripture for resolving guilt: repentance and confession. Repentance (Greek, *metanoia*) is a mental decision that produces an act of the will. When we change our mind about our sin, we do something about that sin. No one ever truly repented and then went on sinning. Confession (Greek, *homologeo*) means to "say the same thing" or "to agree." When we confess, we do not simply declare, "I have sinned." We acknowledge that God's judgment on that sin is just. The Bible promises, "If we confess our sins, he is faithful and just and will forgive us our sins and purify us from all unrighteousness" (1 John 1:9).

The *means*, then, of dealing with guilt is repentance, and the *method* is confession. The *goal* is the freedom of one's conscience. True repentance and confession lead to a clear conscience, which heals the guilty soul. Without a clear conscience, guilt cannot be resolved. Those who refuse to repent of sin will persist in that sin. Those who refuse to confess their sin will pretend things are resolved when they are not. They will never be free from guilt until they face their sin and do something about it.

1. *Acknowledge any hidden personal sin that is the root of your guilt.* Pinpoint wrong attitudes and actions that are eating you up with guilt. Be totally honest with God. He already knows what you have done, "for the LORD searches all hearts, and understands every intent of the thoughts" (1 Chronicles 28:9 NASB). Prayerfully ask the Holy Spirit of God to reveal to you those areas of your life that are not pleasing to God.

2. *Honestly face the sin that is feeding your guilt.* Choose a point at which to clean the slate with God and start over. Do not just admit you have failed. Establish a turning point in your life. Face your sin, confess it, correct it, and forget it. Discard any inferior, irrational, or unbiblical standard you've been comparing yourself to and beating yourself down with. These may be breeding painful false guilt feelings.

3. *Make a complete confession of your sin.* Come to terms with God about the seriousness of your sin. Stop making excuses, and take full responsibility for what you have done. Two marks of genuine confession are *sorrow* according to the will of God and *repentance* without remorse (2 Corinthians 7:10).

4. *Plan to avoid future failure.* See your sin as unwise and self-defeating. Proverbs 8:36 reminds us, "He who sins against me injures himself" (NASB). Realize that tomorrow will be a better day if you conquer sin today. Live to glorify God, not to satisfy yourself. Correcting your problem will bring glory to Him and be an encouragement to others. Totally dedicate yourself to victory.

> *We are guilty before God, yet He who knows us best is willing to forgive and forget and give us another chance.*

Accepting Forgiveness

The Bible assures us only one sin is really *unpardonable*—blasphemy against the Holy Spirit (Matthew 12:31-32). All others may be forgiven! There is nothing you have done that is beyond the reach of God's grace. We must learn to take God's offer of forgiveness seriously. Jesus constantly emphasized that He came to save sinners, not condemn them (John 3:17). By condemning ourselves, we reject God's offer of grace and cleansing. We refuse the only true solution to our problem of guilt.

Salvation is instantaneous, but it initiates a lifelong process. Conversion happens in a split second, but spiritual growth is lifelong. Learning to face our failures and the guilt they produce is part of that process. No one is perfect; no human being is error-free. We are all guilty before God, yet He who knows us best is willing to forgive and forget and give us another chance.

Life's Greatest Fear

One of the greatest causes of depression is dealing with death—your own or that of a loved one. The loss we feel at the point of death can be so overwhelming that its effects can be felt long after a friend or loved one has passed away.

We naturally fear the unknown, and people often fear death more than anything else. We usually fear the death of loved ones more than they do. Even talking about death is difficult for us. Some people fear that facing the reality of death will make them all too aware of the possibility of their own death, so they try to avoid the subject altogether. Yet in trying to avoid discussing death, we instill it with such uncertainty and terror that individuals facing it quite often have trouble dealing with it. In doing so, they usually go through five distinct stages before reaching the stage of final acceptance:

1. Shock/Denial
2. Anger
3. Bargaining
4. Depression
5. Acceptance

Stage 1: Denial or shock. An individual in this stage often refuses to accept the possibility of his or her own death. Repeated trips to different doctors, endlessly repeated tests (in the hopes of better results), refusal to undergo the accepted treatment of a life-threatening illness—all these are symptoms of the denial stage. When facing the reality of their own death, some people throw themselves into frenetic activity, working long hours of overtime or doing endless community-service work. They are trying to deny their own mortality through the wholesale pursuit of vitality and activity.

Stage 2: Anger. After busily futile attempts to undermine the reality of approaching death, people experience feelings of loneliness, guilt, purposelessness, and a real sense of grief. This produces the stage of anger—visible anger. It is not uncommon for terminally ill patients to flare up at their physicians, spouses, neighbors, relatives, and eventually at God Himself.

Stage 3: Bargaining. This is the individual's last effort to escape the now-overwhelming reality of oncoming death. Large gifts to charitable organizations, promises of a change of lifestyle, long lists of new resolutions are all common to the bargaining stage. The length of time spent in this stage depends largely on the patient's ingenuity, energy, and reluctance to think about death.

Stage 4: Depression. The person has now moved past the endless expenditure of energy as seen in the bargaining stage and begins a somber and gradual realization of the consequences of his or her death. Friends or companions are especially important in this stage. Contact with people going through the same experience, participation in terminal patient support groups, quality counseling—all can minimize the despair of this fourth stage of death and dying. In many ways, this stage constitutes a letting go of the fruitless attempt to walk backward in time to a point when death did not seem to be so real. It is here that secular counseling falls so dreadfully short.

Stage 5: Acceptance. For the unbeliever, acceptance is merely a retreat to a fortress of self-reliance. It encompasses the hope of extracting a modicum of final purpose and meaning from the harsh reality of the previous months. For the Christian, however, the stage of acceptance brings a renewed appreciation of the fact that death is merely a transition point, a change of address, if you will, between life in a physical body on this earth to eternal life in a spiritual body in heaven. For the Christian facing death, the Bible's message is one of hope and encouragement.

Accepting the Reality of Death

The Bible reminds us, "Man is destined to die" (Hebrews 9:27). Death is inevitable. It is something to be feared because of what the Scripture calls the "sting of death" (1 Corinthians 15:56). The term in the Greek New Testament *(kentron)* literally means the "stinger of a scorpion." Death is not something people casually accept. The Old Testament tells us people do not want to die because God has "set eternity in the hearts of men" (Ecclesiastes 3:11).

Man has an innate desire for the eternal and can never be fully satisfied by the temporal aspects of life. From the time we are born, we strive to live forever. We want to know the secret to eternal life because we who were created in the image of God sense the reality of life after death.

Life After Death

The Bible clearly teaches there is life after death, for both the saved and the unsaved. To the born-again believer, the Scripture declares that "to be away from the body" is to be "at home with the Lord" (*see* 2 Corinthians 5:8). But to the unsaved it warns, "Multitudes who sleep in the dust of the earth will awake: some to everlasting life, others to shame and everlasting contempt" (Daniel 12:2).

The Bible emphasizes that physical death is not the end of human existence. Man enters a conscious eternity where he faces the possibility of heaven or hell. We make our choice on this side of the grave for either eternal blessing in God's presence or condemnation and exclusion from His presence.

Sometimes we fear death because we get our focus off the eternal and onto the temporal. If you spend your entire lifetime living for the things of this world, you are going to be greatly disappointed, for real life does not consist of the things a person accumulates. Real life is a dynamic fellowship with the living God. If we keep our spiritual focus on eternity, we have every reason to hope and rejoice.

The apostle Paul wrote:

> Listen, I tell you a mystery: We will not all sleep [die], but we will all be changed—in a flash, in the twinkling of an eye, at the last trumpet. For the trumpet will sound, the dead will be raised imperishable, and we will be changed. For the perishable must clothe itself with the imperishable, and the mortal with immortality (1 Corinthians 15:51-53).

The Hope of the Resurrection

Christians have a totally different view of death than non-Christians because they alone know the One who has conquered death itself. Death is "swallowed up" in the victorious resurrection of Jesus Christ (1 Corinthians 15:54). Thus the beloved apostle asks the ultimate questions: "Where, O death, is your victory? Where, O grave, is your sting?" (1 Corinthians 15:55). The reality of death is still present for every one of us, but the sting is gone.

This triumph over death is possible because Christ has already risen for us. "Dust to dust" and "ashes to ashes" holds true only for a while; it is not the final chapter! The Bible declares that though the body perish in the dust, your soul will live forever and you will stand before God on the day of judgment to be received into heaven.

> *To the Christian, death is not something to be feared: It is the first step of a grand entrance into eternal joy and blessing.*

The hope of the resurrection is the reason Paul could say with triumph, "For to me, to live is Christ and to die is gain" (Philippians 1:21). For the apostle, every day was a new and exciting encounter with the risen Christ. Death was just the means of ushering him into the presence of the Savior. Therefore, Paul feared neither life (with all of its complexities) nor death (with all of its uncertainty). To the Christian, death is not something to be feared: It is the first step of a grand entrance into eternal joy and blessing.

Everlasting Life

To the unsaved, death is the ultimate defeat of the human spirit. Man's desire to stay alive is ever threatened by the approaching steps of death. We were born to die. What happens in between our birth and death is the sum and substance of life. Some have called it the "dash" between the dates on a tombstone. That little dash represents the sum and substance of your life.

For the Christian who knows the eternal God, death is only a change of scene, not a change of life. Scripture states, "He who has the Son has life . . ." (1 John 5:12). You do not have to die and go to heaven to obtain everlasting life. The moment you were saved, you became a "partaker of the divine nature" (2 Peter 1:4). You already *have* eternal life right now! Are you living like it?

You can live above the petty human fears of death and aging, recognizing that the eternal God lives within your soul. When you were born again (1 Peter 1:23), your life became co-eternal with the life of God. You will live as long as God will live. So there's no reason to be afraid to die. You have everlasting life in your soul! Why should you fear the sting of death? God has given you eternal life. Your life is co-eternal with His—and you will live forever!

The greatest joy in life is serving the eternal God—the lover of your soul. The greatest fulfillment you will ever find will be in living for Him and cooperating with His eternal plan and purpose for your life. There is no need to fear that which God has already conquered. Where is the sting of death? It was eliminated by the death of Jesus Christ, who put and end to death for everyone who trusts Him as his or her personal Savior!

CHAPTER FIVE

HOW TO GET UP WHEN YOU'RE DOWN

—⁂—

T om moved slowly as he packed the boxes with his personal belongings from the office. He just couldn't believe he had been let go after all those years with the company.

"These things happen," he told Bill. "but I never thought it would happen to me!"

I tried to worn you," Bill responded. "You just weren't getting the job done anymore. I knew all those reprimands were adding up to trouble! I tried to tell you, but you just weren't listening."

Everyone experiences failure sooner or later! Failure is a normal part of human life. It is something we all experience and need to learn how to handle. If we do not deal with failure properly, we will only get bitter and fail again. Human nature is such that when we fail at something, we immediately look for somebody to blame. When Adam sinned in the garden, he blamed both God and Eve for his failure (Genesis 3:12). When Saul failed to fully obey God's instructions, he blamed his sin on the people of Israel (1 Samuel 15:20-22).

The Bible is filled with examples of human failure. Adam condemned the entire human race, yet he was the first person to be saved. Abraham was guilty of lying, adultery, and laughing at God, yet he is remembered as the father of the faithful. Jacob deceived people most of his life, yet became the father of the 12 tribes of Israel. Moses never made it to the promised land, yet he was Israel's greatest leader. Aaron succumbed to idolatry, yet he became God's high priest. Samson fell to Delilah, yet he was Israel's greatest warrior. David committed adultery and murder, yet he was Israel's greatest king. Peter violently denied the Lord, yet he was God's spokesman at Pentecost.

Finding Hope in the Midst of Failure

The first key to growing through failure is realizing that God is greater than your mistakes. Second, failure is a universal part of being human. God wants us to learn from failure. We especially need to learn how not to make the same mistake again. We need to face our weaknesses. Whatever can be changed needs to be changed; wherever we can improve, we need to improve.

If you cannot succeed in a certain area of life, it may very well be that it's not the will of God for you to pursue that area. You might love to play football, but if the doors aren't opening for you to play professionally, then most likely that's not God's calling for your life. You may enjoy singing, but perhaps your voice isn't of the quality that's necessary to be a recording artist. If you aren't achieving the goals you'd like to reach, that doesn't mean you need to feel like a failure. It just means that God intends for you to succeed elsewhere.

Don't let some initial failure cause you to go away discouraged, angry, and upset, or you will never accomplish what you could have had you just kept trying.

What Is Your Definition of Success?

In order to address the problem of failure, we have to start with a question about success. Does God really want us to be successful? There are some pious believers who say, "Oh, the Lord really doesn't intend for us to be successful. We can be failures to the glory of God. The more everything goes wrong, the more spiritual we can become." Then there are those who are bent on success at any cost. Their attitude is, "Do whatever you have to do to succeed, whether it's biblical or not. After all," they rationalize, "God wants us to be successful. He doesn't need any more failures."

But how does God's Word define success? Read Joshua 1:8: "Do not let this Book of the Law depart from your mouth; meditate on it day and night, so that you may be careful to do everything written in it. Then you will be prosperous and successful." By this definition, *success is doing the will of God.* We may think that certain things we do will make God happy with us, but that's not the way it works. Everything we do for God needs to be done *according* to the Word of God in order for it to be done *in* the will of God.

By some standards, Abraham was a total failure. Leaving Ur, the greatest city of his day, he went out to the middle of nowhere to the land of Canaan and there lived and died in obscurity. Yet he is one of the most illustrious men who ever lived. Moses led the slaves of Israel out of Egypt into a wilderness and never entered the Promised Land. He died a failure by modern standards, yet he is one of the greatest men God ever used. Christ died on a cross, initially appearing to be a failure, and yet by His death He won us an eternal victory. For in that death, He atoned for the sins of mankind.

Jesus talked about failure and success in the story of the successful Pharisee and the sinful publican, both of whom went to the temple to pray (Luke 18:9-14). The Pharisee's prayer was boastful—unlike others, he had never let God down. By contrast, the publican stood afar off and bowed his head in humility and prayed, "God, have mercy on me, a sinner." Commenting on this incident, Jesus said, "I tell you that this man [publican] rather than the other [Pharisee], went home justified before God." The man who appeared to be successful was a spiritual failure. The one who appeared to be a failure was the one who was truly successful. Humility, not ability, is the only true success before God.

When people fail, they usually do one of two things. Either they *confess* their failure, repent of it, and get right with God, or they go around making *excuses* for their failure. Those who confess get back on track and ultimately turn their failure into success. The latter never honestly face their failure. They never solve the problems that led to it, and their lives never get turned around. God wants us not only to repent and erase our failure; He wants us to go on and find real success in serving Him.

The Failure Factor

Understanding Failure Orientation

Failure orientation is that self-perception found in some people that limits not only their self-confidence, but even their ability to trust God as all-sufficient Lord. Individuals with a failure orientation are haunted by a sense of failure, which comes from one of two sources:

1. *How we think we appear to others.* If we are prone to a failure orientation, we tend to develop "ears" for negative feedback from others. Blocking out or downplaying positive feedback, the failure orientation makes us morbidly sensitive to any negative response we're getting from others. Unfortunately, we tend to limit the feedback we receive—thereby limiting whatever useful information we might glean from the comments of others. We need feedback from others to help us develop the foundation stones of our value system, self-concept, and understanding of behavior.

Sometimes individuals with a failure orientation have trouble distinguishing between negative feedback directed at them personally and negative feedback simply directed at their behavior. It is important to be able to distinguish between the two in interpreting feedback. "Failure" that may come in the form of a negative response to one's behavior is usually short-lived and may be overcome. Such "failure" should not be mistaken for a negative response to one's own person or self-integrity.

As Christians, we may fail, but we are not failures. No matter what others choose to think of us, we are "more than conquerors" through Jesus Christ, who loves us (*see* Romans 8:37). From time to time, others may praise or ridicule us, but we must never lose our true identity and sense of purpose in the quicksand of struggling to prove ourselves acceptable to others. Scripture describes clearly how we should envision our efforts as we strive to achieve our goals in this life: "Whatever you do, work at it with all your heart, as working for the Lord, not for men. . . . It is the Lord Christ you are serving" (Colossians 3:23-24 NASB).

2. *How we view ourselves.* Frequently, people with a failure orientation have an artificially high, unrealistic, or even perfectionistic set of expectations for themselves. When asked to rate their accomplishments in almost any area on a scale from one to ten, such persons inevitably rate themselves at five or worse. They rate themselves harshly, even when by all objective standards their performance is far above average. These individuals tend to categorically classify themselves as total successes or total failures. They have an "either-or" mentality when viewing their own accomplishments. They see their output as fully acceptable or totally worthless—more often the latter.

Such a sense of failure often paralyzes initiative. These individuals become cautious, diffident, unwilling to take risks their own judgment tells them are perfectly acceptable. Such persons need a comparison group of other individuals who are at a roughly equivalent skill and attribute level with whom they can identify and derive a sense of belonging without either being intimidated or bored.

Overcoming Failure Orientation

How can we overcome failure orientation? Here are some suggestions:

1. *Fully analyze and understand our own failure-prone thinking.* Analyzing the negative thinking and feelings of failure within us can help in identifying the various areas or aspects of life in which they appear. We need to try to delineate these areas as specifically as possible and look for hidden irrational ideas or unbiblical beliefs that serve to undermine our sense of God-given worth.

Usually we can trace our failure orientation back to various setbacks and misconceptions coming from ideas about ourselves, our friends, job, parents, brothers and sisters, church, or school. Rather than perceiving the world through our mind's "failure filter," we need to analyze and approach situations from a biblical perspective. One way to do this is to write down every irrational or unbiblical idea we can pinpoint in our thoughts. Then match it with a passage of Scripture that refutes it.

2. *Choose goals and objectives that will improve our self-concept.* It is advisable to begin with an area in which we have a reasonable amount of self-confidence. A success-oriented self-concept is contagious within our own personality. When we are able to establish goals and begin to reach them, the belief that "I can do all things through Christ Jesus who strengthens me" begins to take on genuine reality in our own experience. From one area of success, this attitude of confident capability will snowball into other personal and professional areas of our lives.

3. *Break the objectives down into bite-sized components.* Once we have begun to take on an objective, it is necessary to approach that goal through a series of small steps. No one can jump from the ground onto the roof of a house, but ten or 12 small steps on a ladder will enable us to get there. By breaking the goal down into a series of smaller bite-sized behaviors and objectives, we simplify our task and heighten our chances for success. These smaller objectives should be undertaken in logical sequence, moving from shortest to longest or easiest to hardest. Here, the wise and thoughtful counsel of a spiritually mature person is invaluable, whether we need advice or just encouragement.

4. *Implement a plan of action.* This is the trial-and-error step. It will involve developing persistence above all else. It will involve the discipline to be well prepared for a task, and sensitivity to remain teachable and flexible. A change in a personal failure orientation of a longstanding nature won't happen overnight. Many times, in fact, we will find ourselves taking two steps forward and one step back, but time is on our side, and the outcome is guaranteed. We can be confident, that "he who began a good work in [us] will carry it on to completion until the day of Christ Jesus" (Philippians 1:6).

Turn Your Failure into Success

Many people never overcome their failures because they never really forgive themselves for failing. They continue to punish themselves with self-inflicted guilt rather than moving beyond failure to success.

1. *To fail is to be human.* All human beings fail. God is fully aware of our limitations: "He knows our frame; He remembers that we are dust" (Psalm 103:14 NKJV). "For all have sinned and fall short of the glory of God" (Romans 3:23). True success is not avoiding failure, but learning what to do with it.

2. *To fail is not be a failure.* Studies show that the most successful people often fail. For example, Babe Ruth not only set the record in his day for home runs in a single baseball season—he led the league in strikeouts, as well. However, that didn't make him a failure. Many Christians who have achieved a number of successes are quick to call themselves failures when they suffer a few strikeouts in life.

3. *No one is ever a failure until he stops trying.* It is better to attempt much and occasionally fail than to attempt nothing and achieve it. No one learns the limits of his ability until he has reached the point of total failure. Thomas Edison tried over 5,000 different types of light-bulb filaments without success before finding one that would work. His willingness to endure many failures without branding himself a failure gave us the electric light.

4. *Failure is never final as long as we get up one more time than we fall down.* Fear is much more damaging than failure. If you've failed, admit it and start over. Forgive yourself and learn to forgive others. Don't be controlled by what has happened to you, but rather be motivated by where you are trying to go. Focus on your goals, not your failures. Move ahead with determination, for nothing worthwhile is accomplished without some risk. "God has not given us a spirit of fear, but of power and of love and of a sound mind" (2 Timothy 1:7 NKJV). God has given you certain gifts and abilities to serve Him. You may not be able to do everything, but you can do something. Go and do it to His glory!

Different Types of Failure

The Divorce Crisis

Every year in the United States, one million marriages end in divorce. Each day, 2,000 teenagers must choose which parent they want to live with. Although parents are often hurt by their married children's decision to divorce, and embittered couples do such harm to each other that they never fully recover, it is the children of divorce who suffer most from a conflict they cannot fully understand.

"I never planned to be divorced," Nancy said. "I didn't think things were that bad. But when Dave walked out—he walked *all* the way out!"

Suddenly Nancy found herself overwhelmed with decisions. She needed to tell the children and her parents. She would have to look for a job and a more affordable place to live. She was beginning to realize that her life would never be the same.

Recent psychological studies have revealed the devastating effects of divorce upon children. Hurt, confusion, alienation, and bitterness are only a few of the deep scars left upon the children of a broken marriage. Millions of American children live with the harsh realities of divorce, and millions more are threatened by the ever-impending possibility of their parents separating.

"But what about the awful results of keeping a bad marriage together?" someone will always ask. In reality, there is no such thing as a bad marriage. Rather, there are badly behaving marriage partners. Marriage is a partnership based upon a relationship. When the partnership goes sour, it is because one or both of the people in it have gone sour. When people fail to relate properly to each other, the marriage suffers.

What the Bible Teaches

The Bible speaks very directly to the issues of marriage, separation, and divorce, and answers some of life's toughest questions: What should I do if I am separated? Is divorce always wrong? What about remarriage? Can God forgive me for a divorce?

Marriage is God's institution. Scripture clearly states that God Himself ordained marriage before the fall (Genesis 2:20-25). God has also revealed His plan of order for the family (Ephesians 5:22-33). Marriage is a divinely ordained institution and is intended to be permanent. Thus, Jesus said, "For this reason a man will leave his father and mother and be united to his wife, and the two will become one flesh. . . . Therefore what God has joined together, let man not separate" (Mark 10:7-9). God intended marriages to last, but they can only survive when both partners are willing to make that possible.

Divorce is the invention of man, not God. Nowhere in Scripture does God ever order divorce. However, He does permit it "because your hearts were hard" (Matthew 19:8). In the Old Testament, divorce was permitted in some cases (Deuteronomy 24:1-4). While some have tried to limit this passage to the divorcing of Jewish engagements only, the context clearly indicates that it is to be applied to the divorcing of a marriage, as well.

In the Law of Moses, remarriage of divorced persons was allowed (though not necessarily encouraged). However, remarriage to one's former partner was clearly disallowed, even in the case of the death of the second partner (Deuteronomy 24:4). God regulated divorce not because He encouraged it, but because hardhearted people were sinning against each other and breaking their marriage vows.

Permission is not promotion. Jesus dealt severely with the matter of divorce because the first-century Jews interpreted Moses' permission as an open promotion of divorce for any reason at all. Thus, our Lord said, "Anyone who divorces his wife, except for marital unfaithfulness (Greek, *porneia*, "sexual sin"), causes her to become an adulteress, and anyone who marries the divorced woman commits adultery" (Matthew 5:32). While Jesus was strict about divorce and the adultery that often resulted from it, He offered forgiveness to the woman taken in adultery (John 8:1-11) and to the five-time-divorced adulteress of Samaria (John 4:3-42).

Marriage is meant to last. The institution of marriage is God's method of stabilizing a sinful society. The family unit is still the basis of our culture, so when the family fails, society and our culture suffer.

God wants the family to succeed; He has given to us, in Scripture, every guideline we need for successful family living. He even promises "righteousness to children's children" if we obey His commandments (Psalms 103:17-18). Your marriage can survive; don't take the easy way out. Be willing to make it work.

When a Separation Occurs

The ideal of Scripture is clearly stated in 1 Corinthians 7:10-11, "A wife must not separate from her husband. . . . And a husband must not divorce his wife." Separations are harmful and hurtful. They leave both partners susceptible to temptation, and they often cause couples to lose all hope of resolving their conflicts. However, there are times when separating becomes unavoidable because of physical or moral harm. Therefore, this same passage states, "But if she does, she must remain unmarried or else be reconciled to her husband" (verse 11).

This passage reveals three definite guidelines for separated couples:

1. *The separated person is not to establish remarriage as a goal of the separation.* Hence, in our present culture, Paul's advice to remain unmarried means do not date. Nothing will hinder a potential reconciliation more than becoming romantically involved with someone else.

2. *The separated couple is to establish reconciliation as their primary goal.* Thus, the task of every Christian counselor is to

help that couple rebuild their marriage in order to prepare for reunion. He must never give up on people, even when they have given up on themselves. It is important to hold out for the possibility of total reconciliation at all times.

3. *The other partner should not seek a divorce to legally end the marriage.* Scripture places a greater responsibility upon the divorcer than the divorcee (Matthew 5:32; Mark 10:11). It is the one who insists upon the divorce who bears the greater guilt. The divorcer is held responsible for his sin and his partner's potential subsequent sin.

When Divorce Occurs

Many people find themselves the victim of a divorce they never wanted. The Bible clearly commands the Christian to remain with an unbelieving mate as a sanctifying influence upon his or her unsaved partner (1 Corinthians 7:12-14). However, there are additional instructions in the event that divorce or adultery occurs.

1. *Desertion by an unsaved partner.* Scripture states, "If the unbeliever leaves, let him do so. A believing man or woman is not bound in such circumstances" (verse 15). While a divorce is usually caused by the behavior of both husband and wife, the Bible indicates that sometimes the divorce is the result of one party's provocation. Scripture definitely states that the believer who is the victim of an unbelieving partner's action is free from the bond of that marriage. The apostle Paul then indicates that if the partner "divorced" in this manner remarries, they have not sinned (verses 27-28), but may have "troubles in this life." They are free to remarry, but may still suffer the scars of the previous marriage. Just because you are *free* to remarry does not mean you are *ready* to remarry.

2. *Adultery by one or both partners.* In the case of adultery, the Bible clearly teaches that divorce is permissible since the marriage vow has been broken and the union violated (Matthew 5:27-32). Yet Scripture is also filled with examples of reconciliation, even after repeated failure. It is clear that adultery does not have to mean the end of a marriage. However, merely going back together and trying to make it work is not enough; there must be a total recommitment to the marriage bond by both parties.

Marriage is a covenant relationship between a man and a woman. When adultery occurs, that covenant is broken. Therefore, the covenant ought to be reestablished and the couple might want to recommit their vows in order to invoke God's blessing on their marriage again. Personal forgiveness may be followed by a formal retaking of the marriage vow, which would officially mark a new beginning for the couple.

3. *Sinful remarriage.* Even when a person has wrongfully, sinfully (unscripturally) divorced and suffers the consequences of that divorce, he or she is still not beyond the possibility of God's forgiveness. There is only one unpardonable sin, and it is not divorce! Therefore, even the sin of divorce can be forgiven. That forgiveness does not excuse divorce; its consequences, even when forgiven, are usually lifelong in their effect.

God's plan for the family is one man for one woman for a lifetime. We must always strive for that ideal as couples and servants of Jesus Christ. Our own marriages ought to reflect the love of Christ for His bride, the church. We must pledge ourselves to learn to love each other, even as Christ loved us with an everlasting love.

How to Prevent Divorce

Divorce is a "decision" that is totally preventable. Of course, because man has a sinful nature, divorce will be a reality until the return of Christ. However, there are ways to minimize the confusion, miscommunication, insensitivity, and divisiveness that so often lead to divorce. The sensitivity survey on page 73 is designed to help improve the quality of communication within the marriage relationship by helping us check our sensitivity to our mate's needs and helping us gather new and meaningful information from our mate's responses.

Marriage Sensitivity Survey

1. What are two things my mate does (or I wish my mate would do) that please me?

   A. _____

   B. _____

2. What are two things I know that I do or could do which please my spouse?

   A. _____

   B. _____

3. What are two qualities in my mate that I admire?

   A. _____

   B. _____

4. What are two things my spouse does that upset or irritate me?

   A. _____

   B. _____

5. What single change in my spouse's behavior would I like to see in the next two weeks? _____

6. What change in my behavior do I think my spouse would like to see in the next two weeks?

   _____

This marriage sensitivity survey is a simple, effective way to take a reading on the quality of communication within a marriage. This survey is designed to be done frequently by each spouse and then discussed together at a convenient, quiet time. I recommend giving adequate time for a good discussion of the responses and praying beforehand that God will give both marriage partners an open, teachable, and non-defensive attitude. In addition, here are some guidelines for improving the quality of communication in marriage:

1. *Be honest with each other.* Stop pretending everything is fine if it is not. Your partner can never make the changes necessary to a happy marriage unless he/she knows you are unhappy.

2. *Be fair with each other.* Stop complaining about the little things. They are only a symptom of deeper frustrations. Get to the heart of the problem, and let your partner do the same with you.

3. *Be firm with each other.* Get tough! Don't give up on each other; that only proves how weak your love is. Show how much you care by making every effort to love and understand each other.

4. *Make time for each other.* Today's dreams are tomorrow's realities. Start dreaming together. Make plans for special times together, and don't let anything interfere. Increase your love by spending time together.

5. *Talk to each other.* Learn to listen with your heart. Open up to each other. Self-disclosure will lead to a more intimate relationship.

6. *Love each other.* Don't take sex for granted. Don't let it get stale and routine. Make time to make love; don't wait until you're too tired. Halfhearted sex will hurt a marriage, and neglect will leave you vulnerable to temptation.

7. *Forgive each other.* Failure is a part of life. There will be times when you fail each other. Learn to forgive and put your mistakes behind you. If you can't forgive together, you'll find it hard to live together.

Living with Divorce

What if you find yourself divorced? A divorce is the end of a marriage, but it is not the end of the world. Life can go on after a divorce; while it's not easy, the situation is not hopeless. Living with the consequences of divorce may not be easy. Guilt, rejection, fear, failure, and anger are all expressions of the agony of divorce. But even when you hurt the most, God has not abandoned you. He still loves you and He still cares about you.

If you are now living as a divorced single parent, determine to be the best parent you possibly can be to your children. You cannot be both dad and mom to them, but you can be an ideal, loving, caring parent who models the character and nature of Christ to them. Divorce is especially difficult for the children. You may not be able to compensate for their pain, but you can certainly bring the love and joy of Christ into their lives.

> *B*ut even when you hurt the most, God has not abandoned you. He still loves you and He still cares about you.

Fear of Rejection

People crave acceptance and fear rejection. Some seek acceptance in business, some in academics, some in athletics. They believe the key to acceptance is success, and they seek success by asserting themselves. Others seek acceptance through interpersonal relationships. Still others have given up looking. They settle for rejection. They reinforce that rejection through depressed behavior patterns such as alcohol or drug abuse.

The lifelong pursuit of acceptance is deeply rooted in human personality. Many people are hungry and searching, without knowing the object of that search. First of all, man has an unquenchable desire to know his Creator. We are all driven by an innate desire for the spiritual and eternal realities of life. We need to know that God accepts us and that He will not reject us. That is why religion is central to man's understanding of himself. Only when you are convinced that God accepts you will you believe that others accept you as well. Most of us fear rejection because we know just how sinful we really are. Acceptance from God thus becomes vital.

Second, man has an innate fear of rejection. Just as the human body has developed immunologic defense systems to resist infectious diseases, so, too, do we develop skills meant to avoid rejection. We will purposely avoid people who have hurt us in the past, and we are careful about sharing with others the personal side of our lives. While none of us expects to be loved by our enemies, we usually become very hurt when a friend turns on us.

The Rejection Syndrome

A life pattern of receiving rejection from early childhood onward can produce *rejection syndrome.* We become so used to rejection that, after a while, we start bringing it on ourselves. Many things can bring on rejection syndrome:

1. *Conditional (performance-based) love.* Some children unconsciously believe they are loved only when they succeed— when they do well in school, sports, music, and so forth.

2. *Unfavorable comparison.* When parents seem to favor one child, the other will feel neglected. While sibling rivalries are normal, selective praise and unfavorable comparison will breed feelings of rejection. No two children are exactly alike in their abilities and interests; that's why comparisons are unfair and unhealthy.

3. *Deprivation of parental love.* Prolonged illness, hospital stays, military service—any of these can separate parents from their children for long periods of time. Consequently, some children come to feel themselves unloved, uncared for. In such cases, a loving parent will do all he or she can to reassure the child.

4. *Divorce.* All children are vulnerable to the tragedy of divorce. Preteens especially tend to blame themselves unjustly, feeling their own worth as a human being has been called into question by the divorce.

5. *Overprotection.* Smothering a child will leave him stifled and unfulfilled. Although usually done with good intentions, overprotective parenting develops unhealthy fears in children. They dread leaving the nest when they grow up.

6. *"Refrigerator" parents.* Some parents genuinely love their children, but cannot express that love verbally or physically. Such coldness will leave the children feeling rejected, perhaps ultimately incapable of expressing love themselves.

7. *Child abuse.* The ultimate form of rejection is mental or physical abuse. The unwanted child detects his parents' rejection easily, as do some handicapped children.

8. *Teenage rejection.* The adolescent is the most vulnerable to social rejection. Teens who feel rejected by their peers form personality patterns that often last a lifetime. Their fear of rejection makes them either blind conformists or willful eccentrics.

9. *Young-adult insecurity.* Rejected teens grow up to be insecure young adults. They usually have trouble making friends with the opposite sex. Their closest friends also tend to be social outcasts. Their fear of rejection often spurs them to bizarre behavior that only brings further rejection.

10. *Adult dysfunction.* When adolescents and young adults fail to find security and acceptance, their personality failings as adults become glaringly obvious. They are prone to failure both at home and at work, which only deepens their sense of not belonging.

Acceptance Begins with God

Hell is the ultimate rejection—perpetual exclusion from God's presence. Yet God does not want to reject people. To avert that punishment, He poured out His wrath on His Son. He nailed our sins to the cross. The penalty has been paid; no barriers stand between us and God. Sinful and thankless as we are, He offers us His love and acceptance.

Scripture tells us the believer is an adopted and accepted child of God (Ephesians 1:5-6). We are accepted by God's love, forgiven by His grace, and transformed by His Spirit. Christ is in God, and we are in Christ. Thus, through our spiritual union with Him, we are secure. Our acceptance is based not on performance, but on our relationship with Him. Since the Father is satisfied with Christ's sacrifice for our sins, He accepts us totally as His children. Because of the atonement on the cross, our debt is canceled and we are new creations in Christ Jesus (2 Corinthians 5:17).

Overcoming Rejection

While our experiences of rejection during childhood may have ingrained in us the belief that we're failures, it's possible to overcome such a perspective. We do not need to remain a victim of our past. Here's the alternative:

1. *Accept God's love.* Stop running from the God who loves you. Accept His forgiveness; claim His acceptance!

2. *Stop rejecting yourself.* In Christ you are a child of God. Stop denying your sonship. You are a joint heir with Jesus. Act like it! Self-rejection denies your new identity in Christ.

3. *Stop blaming others.* While other people may have rejected you, you don't need to reject yourself as well. Don't let rejection become an attitude within yourself, and don't blame your condition on everybody else.

4. *Start living like a child of the King.* Jesus said that He would not reject whoever would come to Him (John 6:37). You are fully and completely accepted by God in Christ. You are a member of God's family. While your present circumstances may hurt, they are temporary. From an eternal perspective, you have a great future ahead of you.

Amazing Grace!

God's grace is sufficient for all your failures. He loves you as much as you will ever be loved. God can't love you more than He already does, and He won't love you less, no matter what. You are His child—now and forever. But His love is not an excuse for us to take advantage of His grace. We are responsible for our own actions and their consequences in our lives. God's grace assures us that He will still be there to help us even when we struggle with life's toughest problems.

CHAPTER SIX

WHEN YOU JUST CAN'T TAKE IT ANYMORE

—◊—

N o one can escape pressure; it affects everyone. Under pressure, one of two things always happens: We find ourselves strengthened and fortified from within (like a diamond), or we crack (like an egg). How we *handle* pressure will determine whether we stand or break.

"That's it! I've had it!" Janet screamed at her children. "You have gone too far this time and I'm not going to put up with this anymore," she exploded. "This is the last time you will ever have a friend over for the night!"

"But Mom," Jennifer cried, "it's the first time anybody has ever been here!"

Pressure begins in the mind. It is a result of how we think about ourselves and our responsibilities. Some people feel more pressure than others in the same situation because they look at life differently. And finally, people handle pressure differently. One may talk out his frustrations, while another finds relief only in pushing himself to his limits.

Causes of Pressure

The greatest cause of pressure is the individual himself. You pressure yourself by how you respond to the demands on your life. Therefore, learning to handle pressure involves learning how to deal with your attitude toward yourself.

1. *Self-identity.* Our own self-concept often makes us push ourselves. If we view ourselves as superman or superwoman, our goal will be success at all costs. We will shrink from the slightest thought of failure. A poor self-concept, on the other hand, makes us dread even the smallest challenge.

2. *Goals.* Sometimes we suffer undue pressure because we set unrealistic goals for ourselves and then suffer agony when we fail to reach them. We become irritable and upset at the slightest obstacle. We need to turn these goals over to God. We need to surrender our plans to Him and make sure they are, in fact, *His* plans.

3. *Fear.* Fear is a major cause of stress. It distracts our gaze from the Almighty God and turns it onto our own scanty resources. Fear of failure in one situation actually causes greater fear in another. The more we fear, the more anxious we become, until we crack under pressure. Fear drives us away from people and responsibility. While it can at times be self-protecting, it can also be self-destructive.

4. *Time.* One of the greatest pressures on people today is a lack of time. Whenever we feel oppressed by a lack of time, we are trying to do too much! Today people accomplish more in one day than their ancestors did in a week or even a month. The hurried pace of life nowadays makes us tackle more than we could possibly do. Age is also a factor. We may have been able to push ourselves 18 hours a day at age 25, but at age 50, we may need to slow down.

5. *Health.* Many times we drive ourselves hard without making allowances for sickness. Have you ever felt you simply had no time to be sick? When we take on a ruthless pace, usually an illness of some kind becomes inevitable—laying us up not just for days, but weeks and months. If we sense some danger signals from our body, we should readjust our priorities and try to get more rest.

6. *Family.* Family problems bring some of the greatest pressures of all. Working men and women are often under stress on the job because things are not going well at home. What's important to realize is that a healthy home helps to relieve our stress levels at work. If we take the time to succeed at home, we are more likely to succeed at work.

7. *Finances.* Financial mismanagement is a major cause of pressure. Being in debt saps our mental and emotional strength. Monetary problems can be corrected only with time, trouble, and effort.

Self-induced Conflict

The most common cause of most pressure is irresponsibility. When we fail to manage our time, health, family, and finances properly, we only add further pressure on ourselves when that mismanagement catches up with us. If you over-schedule yourself on a given day, you will be under pressure almost immediately and stay frustrated all day long.

The real inner conflict of self-induced pressure is our struggle against God's sovereignty. We are actually at war against His will for our lives. When we schedule ourselves too tightly, or push ourselves too hard, we are trying to do more than God intends us to. All the pressure and conflict we suffer comes from seeking what we want, not what He wants.

Learning to accept our God-given limitations is just as important as learning to accept our God-given gifts and abilities. When we attempt to do more than God has planned for us, we will experience pressure. Therefore, learning to handle pressure means learning to focus on our God-given priorities and saying no to everything else.

Conquering Pressure

Wishing a problem would go away never makes it go away. Action is required on our part:

1. *Surrender.* Stop fighting God. Your agenda is not His agenda if it is crushing you. While some pressure is normal in life, you cannot continually go from one pressure-packed situation to another without cracking. Surrender your goals to do His will.

2. *Pray.* Learn to release pressure through prayer. When you talk to God, you are talking to the sovereign Lord of the universe. True prayer will conquer worry and fear. Take your pressures to the Lord and get His direction.

3. *Talk.* Find someone who understands what you are going through and talk it out with him or her. While talking will not solve the problem, it will certainly release some of your tension. Do not be afraid to talk to your husband or wife, pastor, counselor, or friend.

4. *Play.* Some pressure can be released through physical recreation. Some people break down because they get little or no physical exercise. Taking time to exercise will give you more quality time to work. Jog, hike, bowl, swim, bike, sail, write—whatever. Get out and go. You'll be glad you did.

5. *Plan.* Start planning your work and activities to allow time for pressure release. Don't push yourself so hard or schedule yourself so full that you have no time to pray, meditate, or even reminisce. Leave yourself room to grow and develop as a human being.

We all have great potential, but we can realize it only by doing what God has really called us to do.

Confronting Life's Crises

We hear much today about people having a midlife crisis. Our relentless pursuit of success and material prosperity has given us a burned-out society. Millions of people enter their forties and fifties and find themselves adrift, without purpose or direction. And many who are younger are restless and uncertain about whether they've really found their calling in life. Whatever our age, if we feel aimless, we will find ourselves tempted to ...

1. *Go back*—retreat to childhood or adolescence in search of peace and security. We will find ourselves daydreaming, brooding about "lost time," wondering what might have been, and doubting our future.

2. *Go under*—collapse under the pressures of life. We cannot concentrate—our lives become aimless. Introspection, sudden emotional outbursts, and deep depression are symptoms. Drug use, alcoholism, and sexual infidelity are very common at this point as false "escape mechanisms" from the pressures of mid-life crisis.

What we really need to do in every crisis is *move ahead.* Face our pressure, reevaluate our priorities, reduce our agenda. We need to determine how much we can reasonably handle. We need to get a fresh start—get out of our rut and tackle something new. It's better for us to recapture our full potential by doing a few things well rather than a lot of things poorly. We all have great potential, but we can realize it only by doing what God has really called us to do.

When You're Overtired

In an age of so much leisure, it is remarkable that so many thousands of Americans are chronically tired. Unfortunately, this is true for Christians, too.

All the possible causes of excessive fatigue or exhaustion are too numerous to mention here, but ask yourself if any of the following statements apply to you:

- "I am so wiped out at the end of the day that it's all I can do to change and collapse into bed."
- "I feel more exhausted in the morning when I wake up than when I go to bed at night."

- "I feel so drained of energy lately that I am barely able to get the necessities done at home or at the office."

The Causes of Fatigue

If any of those statements apply to you, then you'll want to consider the following four causes of fatigue:

1. *Physical causes of fatigue.* Physical overexertion can be a cause of chronic fatigue. However, in twentieth-century America, this is very rare. By far the most common physical cause of fatigue in this country is underexertion. Our bodies were designed by God to take in food for energy, metabolize that food through strenuous physical effort, excrete the wastes, and rest appropriately. All this was intended to produce a healthy bodily "temple" in which the spirit of man and the Spirit of God could co-dwell.

As man's technological ingenuity has increased, however, so has his ability to avoid exertion. Therefore, our physical bodies are often underused. Imagine buying a powerful sports car and never driving it more than five miles an hour, creeping back and forth to work and on errands. Eventually it would begin to sputter, misfire, and have trouble getting started. Such is the physical condition of many people. Regular and strenuous exercise—under the supervision of your family physician—is the key to overcoming the most common physical cause of fatigue—under-exertion.

2. *Pathological causes for fatigue.* Pathological causes for fatigue are those that result from any physical illness or disorder. It is quite common after a major illness or surgical procedure to feel fatigued or burned out for several weeks. While recuperating, you should pace yourself and not rush back into full activity too soon. Otherwise you will only prolong your period of recovery. You may even suffer a relapse.

Extended fatigue that lasts for several weeks, with no apparent physical cause and no real relief, should be cause for concern and requires a thorough medical checkup. Chronic fatigue associated with any of the following symptoms should be investigated by your doctor as soon as possible, for these symptoms are widely known as cancer's seven warning signals:

- Change in bowel or bladder habits
- A sore that does not heal
- Unusual bleeding or discharge
- Thickening or lump in breast or elsewhere
- Indigestion or difficulty in swallowing
- Obvious change in wart or mole
- Nagging cough or hoarseness

3. *Psychological causes for fatigue.* General practitioners readily admit that nearly 50 percent of the people who visit their offices with "physical" complaints really suffer from emotional disorders. Emotional problems, especially depression, anxiety, and worry, are by far the most common causes of extended fatigue. The body's fatigue-resistance system can, in time, be worn down by continual emotional and personal stress.

The body has a tremendous ability to adjust to different situations and different pressures, but prolonged emotional unrest—generated by either internal psychological conflict or external situational stress—can lead to anatomical and physical changes in the body which produce fatigue, exhaustion, and often disease. Modern medical science is only beginning to understand the real and important link connecting our emotional state and our physical well-being.

4. *Spiritual causes of fatigue.* The Bible clearly teaches that man's spiritual and physical well-being are closely connected. Guilt-impenitent, continual sin often lies at the root of bodily sickness or fatigue. In Psalms 32:3 we read, "When I was silent about my sin, my body began to waste away, and I found myself groaning all the day long" (author's paraphrase). The anxiety produced by continual or unconfessed sin can wear us down, leaving us tired and dispirited as we try to go about the business of living.

Five Cures for Fatigue

1. *Maintain a clear conscience.* Scripture teaches that when a believer is involved in continual and unrepentant sin, his prayers are ineffective before the Lord. Our anguish and isolation will, in turn, foster unremitting anxiety—an anxiety cured only by confession and the restoration of a right relationship with God. King David, in the Old Testament, understood the necessary healing power of such a relationship. He wrote, "I acknowledged my sin to you and did not cover up my iniquity. I said, 'I will confess my transgressions to the LORD,' and you forgave the guilt of my sin" (Psalm 32:5).

2. *Eat a well-balanced diet.* A well-balanced diet depends on both the quantity and the quality of the food we eat. Three meals a day are best, at regular intervals. Early in the morning, eat something low in sugar but high in protein. Small amounts of caffeine, a cup of coffee, for instance, are acceptable, but you should never perk yourself up with coffee or sweets while omitting regular, well-balanced meals. Quick "pick-me-up" foods, gobbled up at odd hours, and occasional binge meals throughout the week, generally put on extra pounds. These, of course, are an added burden to the cardiovascular, respiratory, muscular, and skeletal systems of the human body, and they produce fatigue, too. The weight charts on page 88 should help you determine whether you're carrying extra weight that may be contributing to a sense of fatigue.

Not only is it important *how much* we eat; we should pay attention to *what* we eat. Americans usually have no trouble eating enough—or more than enough—protein. However, there are six essential vitamin groups our bodies can run low on, contributing to a sense of physical fatigue and loss of stamina.

- *Vitamin A.* Vitamin A is easily depleted by stress; it is necessary both for healthy skin and clear night vision. Foods that contain plenty of vitamin A are liver, apricots, carrots, yellow squash, egg yolk, butter, and cream.

- *Vitamin B complex.* The B vitamins are the body's "energy transfer" vitamins. They allow the body to utilize the calories it takes is for proper maintenance of function and growth. The vitamin B complex is also essential to the proper function and growth of the nervous system, and significant shortage of any of the B complex vitamins can lead not only to fatigue but to emotional symptoms consistent with depression. The B complex vitamins are widely available in wheat germ, eggs, pork, brewer's yeast, nuts, potatoes, legumes, and liver.

- *Vitamin C.* Vitamin C has been recognized as essential in the body's defense against infections. There is also some evidence that vitamin C, especially when taken in fresh fruits, may help retard hardening of the arteries—a condition usually caused by the buildup of cholesterol in the small blood vessels. Potatoes, cabbage, green peppers, tomatoes, and virtually all fruits are high in vitamin C.

- *Vitamin D.* Vitamin D is essential to the proper absorption and utilization of both phosphorus and calcium. For this reason, it is often added to the milk we buy commercially. Calcium and phosphorus are necessary for the repair and strengthening of bones. Butter, egg yolk, liver, and cod liver oil are rich sources of vitamin D.

- *Vitamin E.* Vitamin E has been connected to the proper healing of wounds and may offer some protection against heart disease. Foods such as margarine, legumes, egg yolk, vegetable oil, and wheat germ are rich in vitamin E.

- *Vitamin K.* Vitamin K is especially necessary for the proper health of the blood. Its main function is to ensure that the blood clots properly and can, therefore, circulate through our bodies without hemorrhaging. Should we sustain cuts or bruises, it is essential that the blood clot properly. Vitamin K is richly available in leafy vegetables, vegetable oil, and pork liver.

Men Age 25 and Older

Height	Small Frame	Medium Frame	Large Frame
5'1"	109-117	115-126	123-138
5'2"	112-120	118-130	126-141
5'3"	115-123	121-133	129-145
5'4"	118-126	124-136	132-149
5'5"	120-130	127-140	135-153
5'6"	125-134	131-144	139-158
5'7"	129-138	135-149	144-163
5'8"	133-142	139-153	148-167
5'9"	137-147	143-157	152-171
5'10"	141-151	147-162	156-176
5'11"	145-155	151-167	161-181
6'0"	149-159	155-172	165-186
6'1"	153-164	159-177	170-191
6'2"	157-168	164-182	175-196
6'3"	161-172	169-187	179-201

Women Age 25 and Older

Height	Small Frame	Medium Frame	Large Frame
4'8"	90-96	94-105	102-117
4'9"	92-99	96-108	104-120
4'10"	94-102	99-111	107-123
4'11"	97-105	102-114	110-126
5'0"	100-108	105-117	113-129
5'1"	103-111	108-120	116-132
5'2"	106-114	111-124	119-136
5'3"	109-117	114-128	123-140
5'4"	112-121	118-133	127-144
5'5"	116-125	122-137	131-148
5'6"	120-129	126-141	135-154
5'7"	124-133	130-145	139-156
5'8"	128-138	134-149	143-161
5'9"	132-142	138-153	147-166
5'10"	136-146	142-157	151-171

Individuals between the ages of 18 and 25 years should subtract one pound for each year under 25 years of age to arrive at their projected ideal weight.

3. *Get regular exercise.* Not only does regular exercise help you do physical labor without getting tired, it actually helps you to think better. You will need to choose the best time of day for exercising—that time varies from person to person. For some people, an early morning regimen is the best—one that leaves them braced and ready to meet the day. Others, if they can, exercise during the middle of the day, preferring a noon workout to simply sitting during lunch. Probably the most popular time is the late afternoon and early evening. People use that time to unwind both mentally and physically after a hard day's work on the job or at home. Ask your doctor how much exercise, and what kind, would be best for you. Any regular fitness program should produce the following:

- Better cardiovascular function (stronger heart and increased blood circulation)
- Lower blood pressure
- Reduced levels of cholesterol and fats in the blood
- Increased muscle size and strength. This will also increase bone strength over time and check your bones' tendency to lose calcium with advancing age
- Reduction of excessive body fat
- Increased physical stamina—you will be able to work longer at peak capacity, even speeding up under pressure
- Recent experimental research suggests that being physically fit helps you both to concentrate better and remember better. That's exactly what many joggers say: The time they spend running helps to clear their head and helps them to concentrate better when they get back to work

4. *Pace yourself.* Save the hardest jobs for your peak times. Some people work best in the late afternoon. Others claim to be night people and do their best work in the late evening. Still others, who are morning people, are at their best during the first few hours of the day. To some extent, of course, the laws of the marketplace dictate when we may or may not tackle certain jobs.

5. *Vacations, breaks, and sleep.* All three are different ways both mind and body can rest and recuperate. You should take vacations when you most need them. In America, unfortunately, they are often more hectic and rigorously planned than regular jobs. Regular breaks taken throughout the day—a brisk walk or a friendly chat with a colleague—will often reduce fatigue and make you more productive.

Proper sleep is crucial in avoiding fatigue and depends, in turn, on how fit you are, both physically and emotionally. Don't turn to narcotics like alcohol or sleeping pills, which only become less effective after time. God's original plan—work six days and rest one—still works. If you live right, work right, eat right, and sleep right, you will feel right. Exercise, watch your diet, and you will start to feel better immediately.

If you want to feel better and live longer, then exercise! There is no substitute for a regular physical workout to keep you trim and fit. Just walking 30–60 minutes a day will "jump start" your body and revitalize your inner being.

All Upset over Nothing

A certain university professor taught a class on preaching. Weekends he drove down to Georgia to pastor a small church. One day he came into class a little discouraged and upset. Departing from his lecture, he explained that this small church seated about 150 people and had an aisle running down the middle.

"You will never believe this," he said, "but after being there for several weeks, I've noticed the same people tend to sit on the same side of the church. Though they move around on their side, they never seem to change sides. Finally, this past weekend when I arrived, I asked one of the deacons, 'Why do these people always sit on this side and those people always sit on the other side?' Taking me into the auditorium, he pointed at the carpeting that ran down the aisle and under the pews. I'd never paid much attention to it before, but suddenly I realized there was a seam where two pieces of carpeting fit together. Then I realized that one side was just a shade lighter blue than the other. The deacon looked at me. 'Preacher,' he said, 'the people who voted for the light shade sit on this side, and the people who voted for the dark shade sit on the other side.'"

Someone in the preacher's class asked, "Well, what are you going to do about it?"

He replied, "I'm going to get a carpenter in there and tear the whole thing out and put in a *red* rug."

It turned out nobody liked the red rug, but they finally began to change sides!

Learning to Lean on God

All too often, we let ourselves become divided over the most petty things that God isn't concerned about at all! The Bible makes it clear that God's real concern is for His children—that they love one another and get along with one another. The Bible also teaches that conflict will always be a part of our lives (Luke 17:1). We are warned, however, not to be the *source* of the conflict. All too often we make the situation worse by the selfish manner in which we respond to conflict. Instead of relying on Him, we take the matter into our own hands.

God's purpose in allowing problems to come into our lives is far more important than our personal convenience. He allows us to suffer through interpersonal conflicts for our own good. Conflicts keep us humble, build patience, and develop our spiritual character. However, if we react negatively, we defeat the purpose of the conflict and end up having to repeat the lesson. If we miss the whole point of whatever God may be trying to say, He may allow more conflict. That is what the Bible means when it says, "God opposes the proud, but gives grace to the humble" (James 4:6). God never allows us to be completely defeated when we are humbled and teachable before Him. It is then that we experience His grace. It is then that He reaches down and meets us at the point of our deepest need.

But until then, we often do not even look for the reaching hand of God to meet our needs. We neglect that outpouring of

His grace upon our lives day after day, forgetting that God can take the *worst* of conflicts and produce the *best* of results to His glory and to our benefit. We need to grow and come to that point of spiritual maturity where we do not let ourselves get defeated by every little problem that comes along.

> *R*emember, God is greater than your greatest problem. He can overrule the worst of problems in order to produce the best of results.

Remember, God is greater than your greatest problem. He can overrule the worst of problems in order to produce the best of results. He knows what our greatest needs are, and He stands ready to meet them. God wants us to develop assertive and positive responses to the conflicts of life (as illustrated on page 80-81).

Cooperating with His Plan

We cannot let conflict stunt our spiritual growth and hinder God's work in our life. If we let a problem get too big it could easily keep us from the joy of our salvation. Remember that Romans 8:28 still applies to us: "We know that all things work together for good to those who love God, to those who are the called according to His purpose" (NKJV). God has a wonderful plan for our life, and when we cooperate with that purpose, we will see beautiful results.

Scripture reminds us that when we were saved, we became heirs of God and joint heirs with Jesus Christ. We receive not only the blessings of His Spirit but whatever else belongs to a son or daughter of the Most High. He does for us what we could never do for ourselves! It's no wonder, then, that this passage ends by saying, "Who shall separate us from the love of Christ? Shall trouble or hardship or persecution or famine or nakedness or danger or sword? . . . No, in all these things we are more than conquerors through him who loved us" (Romans 8:35,37).

The victory has already been won! We need only learn how to appropriate it. We need to choose an assertive response, not an aggressive or passive one, to the conflicts of life. It takes faith to act assertively on the promises of God's Word when dealing with the people, problems, and situations of this life. But God states that His eyes search the world over, seeking to help those believers who are willing to take Him at His Word and walk in faith (2 Chronicles 16:9).

Doing Things Right

Solving conflicts involves decision-making. Problems rarely go away on their own. We must decide that we want to resolve the conflict. We must usually take corrective action in order to eliminate a conflict. Assertive action, based on biblical principles, is necessary if a conflict is going to be resolved. Learn how to tackle the problem God's way. If you will do what is right, He will bless your efforts.

Finally, remember that the opposite of conflict is fellowship. Only when conflict ceases can fellowship be restored. Don't wait for the other person to come to you. Instead, go to him or her, lovingly and kindly, to seek reconciliation as soon as possible. Do it today!

Biblical Response Chart

The Causal Situation	The Passive Response *This is not a biblical response* (1 Corinthians 16:13; Colossians 2:5)	The Aggressive Response *This is not a biblical response* (John 13:35; Romans 12:17)	The Assertive Response *This is a biblical response* (1 Peter 5:9; 1 Thessalonians 5:14)
In situations where the Christian encounters major personal trials.	"God cares little for me, or at least He doesn't act like He does."	"People get what they deserve and God is the judge who makes that decision."	"God is just in all He does, but He tempers that justice with mercy and compassion, encouraging us to grow into the likeness of Christ."
In situations where the Christian is the target of unfair or unacceptable actions by others.	"I'll just act like nothing happened, and try to be cheery."	"Try that again and you'll wish you hadn't; don't tread on me!"	"A problem has developed between us, and I know you'll agree that we've got to honestly face it and resolve it as soon as possible."
In situations that call for the Christian to show sensitive compassion toward another person.	"I care only for you and I will not accept myself unless I can make you happy."	"I am not the kind of person who shows the weakness of emotional sensitivity."	"I understand your hurting and needs, and I will respond with compassion and personal strength to help as best I can."
In situations where the Christian must team up with another person to accomplish a task.	"I am willing to completely throw myself into meeting your expectations and I will feel guilty if I don't."	"I expect you to perform up to my expectations and standards. I will accept no less."	"I am responsible for my behavior and will offer you the opportunity to take responsibility for your actions. Together we can effectively serve the Lord."
In situations that require the Christian to show open and vulnerable communication.	"I am unwilling to voice opinions which might upset you, and I will keep nothing private in my life."	"I know what is best for you and I will accept you only if you agree with my opinion."	"I value you and your opinions. I will be honest with you and will appreciate your being honest with me as we seek to genuinely communicate."

CHAPTER SEVEN

WHEN YOU'RE TEMPTED TO GIVE UP

—⟁—

B ob and Tonya had been married for six years when she told him she was leaving. He was shocked and devastated.

"What's wrong?" he pleaded.

"Everything!" Tonya snapped back. "I just can't live like this anymore."

"What can I do?" Bob asked desperately.

"I don't know," she replied. "I give up!"

It turned out later that Tonya had already fallen in love with someone else. Her inability to love Bob was precipitated by a disastrous affair with yet another person.

Ever since the days of Adam and Eve, man has been tempted. Your battle with temptation is not unique to you. It is a universal problem.

The Source of Temptation

One of the major reasons people cannot handle the problem of temptation is their refusal to face the real source of their temptation: themselves! We must face the fact that we are our own worst enemies. The real source of temptation is neither God nor Satan. In most cases, temptation begins in one's own heart as we are enticed to give in to our own desires. All too often, the Christian believer refuses to admit to himself that he is toying with sin—until it is too late.

Don't Blame the Devil

The easiest way to avoid any personal responsibility regarding our own sin is to blame it on the devil. Many people claim that they cannot deal with their temptation because "the devil made me do it."

One well-meaning lady told her counselor that she really didn't yell and scream at her husband. "The devil makes me do it," she insisted.

Her counselor replied, "I can't make the devil stop yelling at your husband, but I can appeal to make *you* stop."

Remember, Satan is not omnipresent; he is a limited, created being. Chances are that Satan has never dealt with you personally. Also, a believer is no longer under Satan's control. While he may trouble you from without (and that only by God's permission— *see* Job 1:12), he no longer has a claim over your life. His power has been broken by the victorious death and resurrection of Christ. Try as he might, Satan cannot enter your mind and possess your will, thoughts, or emotions.

It took the counselor nearly 20 minutes to convince this woman that she was indeed responsible for yelling at her husband. Finally she burst into tears: "You're right, I did it! I yelled at him myself!"

"Good," the counselor replied. "You see, we can stop your husband from aggravating you, and we can get you to stop yelling at him, but we can't make the devil stop."

Don't Blame God

When we are in despair about our frustrations, we may be tempted to blame God for our problems. We may say, *Why is God doing this to me?* However, the Bible clearly teaches that God is not the author of temptation: "When tempted, no one should say, 'God is tempting me.' For God cannot be tempted by evil, nor does he tempt anyone" (James 1:13).

God may allow Satan to tempt us, but even then, the Bible promises that "God is faithful; he will not let you be tempted beyond what you can bear" (1 Corinthians 10:13). There is no excuse, then, for failure or defeat. Should we fail, we have only ourselves to blame. If God let temptation come to men such as Abraham, Job, Moses, David, and Paul, why should we expect to be exempt?

The Battle Begins in Your Mind

The Bible tells us plainly that what we think (Greek = *logizomai*) not only determines how we live, but reflects who we are. "For as [a man] thinketh in his heart, so is he" (Proverbs 23:7 KJV). Every Christian knows what it is to be enslaved to lust, hatred, greed, jealousy, or envy. All of these are poison to the soul. Recognizing this, the apostle Paul wrote:

> Finally, brothers, whatever is true, whatever is noble, whatever is right, whatever is pure, whatever is lovely, whatever is admirable—if anything is excellent or praiseworthy—think about such things (Philippians 4:8).

Seven guidelines will help you clean up your thought life:

1. *Admit that you have a problem.* Rationalizing sin will never cure it. Whatever sinful thoughts we are troubled with, we must confess them to God. Be honest with Him who searches our hearts and minds and knows our thoughts. Read 2 Samuel 12 or Psalm 51—and learn the importance of laying your sin before God.

2. *Believe that God can make a difference in your thought life.* There are no doubting victorious Christians. In Hebrews 11:6 we learn that without faith we cannot please God; if we are to approach Him for strength or wisdom, we must believe Him capable of supplying it. "Blessed be the Lord, who daily bears our burden, the God who is our salvation. God is to us a God of deliverances" (Psalm 68:19-20 NASB).

3. *Take a long, hard look at yourself.* God gives no blessing to Christians who hold out on Him. "If I regard wickedness in my heart, the Lord will not hear" (Psalm 66:18 NASB). If we want our minds renewed, we must be painfully honest—both with God and ourselves. Search out and confess those thoughts that displease Him.

4. *Make a 100-percent commitment.* There must come a point when we are revolted at our own vileness. It is at this point that God wants the Christian to resolve to "go all the way with God's way." This means conforming every thought to the holiness enjoined in Scripture. David put it this way:

> "Your word is a lamp to my feet and a light to my path. . . . I will follow your righteous laws. . . . My heart is set on keeping your decrees to the very end" (Psalm 119:105-106, 112).

5. *Be flexible and willing to change.* Jesus likened a stagnant Christian to an old wineskin—no longer flexible, incapable of holding new wine. Christians who have become narrow-minded, stale, and complacent are especially vulnerable to un-Christlike thoughts. These we must set aside. God's goal for us is the perfect holiness exemplified in His Son.

6. *See God as the only refuge.* We live in a society geared to human pride and self-sufficiency. Even Christians sometimes forget that only God is our true deliverer. David acknowledged as much, saying, "The help of man is worthless . . ." (Psalm 60:11), and "Pour out your hearts to him, for God is our refuge" (Psalm 62:8).

7. *Renewal is a full-time job.* Romans 12:2 teaches that we are "transformed by the renewing of our minds." But we must be vigilant. A daily quiet time in the Word is essential. Are you often troubled by an unclean thought? Find the appropriate Scripture and quote it to yourself when that thought comes around again. Start memorizing Scripture—maybe three or four verses every week. Learn to meditate on Scripture, asking the Holy Spirit for aid and illumination. Ask God to reveal His attributes to you. Seek to know Him in every thought and deed.

Follow through on these seven guidelines, and you will find your thinking more and more Christlike. Much is at stake here. You can choose either to cleanse your mind with God's Holy Word, or surrender it to unclean thoughts prompted by Satan, God's adversary and ours.

Experiencing Victory over Temptation

First Corinthians 10 opens by reminding us how the Israelites were tempted in the wilderness. God was not pleased with them, and they were "scattered over the desert" (verse 5). The apostle Paul then goes on to tell us that these things happened for our example (verses 6-10). Therefore, we should take warning and not:

- Lust
- Be idolaters
- Commit fornication
- Tempt Christ
- Murmur

The first step in conquering temptation is to face our sin and its terrible consequences. All too often, we try to rationalize away the seriousness of sin and thereby fall victim to its clutches. Sin is no laughing matter with God. It is rebellious disobedience to His law. If we will follow God's prescription for conquering temptation, we can keep ourselves from falling into sin.

1. *Admit to yourself that you are being tempted.* Acknowledge your feelings. Face your temptation head-on and determine to *do* something about it!

2. *Confess to God that you are tempted to sin.* We are not only to confess our sins to God, but even the very fact that we *desire* to sin. Remember that God sees everything you are doing, and He knows everything you are thinking (*see* Psalm 139:2). Run to Him in prayer and ask for His help now, before you sin.

3. Seek the help of a Christian friend. Two kinds of friends are to be avoided: the harsh, censorious type and the over-lenient type. Go to someone who will help you turn from sin without turning from you. Ask to pray with that person. The Bible reminds us that we are to "carry each other's burdens" (Galatians 6:2).

4. There are no excuses for failure. The Bible promises, "No temptation has seized you except what is common to man" (1 Corinthians 10:13). Others have won out over temptation; why should you be an exception? Sin is sin. Stop thinking about what to do, or why you are feeling overwhelmed, and decide to do what you know is right! "Resist the devil, and he will flee from you" (James 4:7).

5. Trust God to give you the victory. He is faithful! If you really believe that, you will deal with your temptation by making "no provision for the flesh." You cannot expect God to help you when, at the same time, you are preparing to disobey Him.

6. Take the "way of escape"! Get away from the source of your temptation. Don't try to get as close as you can to temptation. Get as far away from it as possible!

When Suffering Comes

Betty was an outstanding wife and mother and a devoted Christian. But her final days of battling cancer were heartbreaking. She gasped for every breath in those final moments of her life. You couldn't watch her suffer without asking, "Why?"

One of the most difficult temptations to handle is that of suffering. Whenever we believe we are suffering unjustly, we will be tempted to question God's grace and wisdom in our lives.

The Bible makes it clear that it is not always God's will to heal our infirmities. Rather, Scripture emphatically states that God uses suffering to develop certain qualities in our lives. The apostle Paul was familiar with suffering and grief; in 2 Corinthians 1:3-4 he refers to the Lord as the "God of all comfort, who comforts us in all our troubles, so that we can comfort those who are in any trouble." Here we see a purpose behind suffering: Our troubles enable us to help others.

Suffering Has Meaning

In God's dealings with His children, no suffering is meaningless. For the Christian believer, "in all things God works for the good of those who love him, who have been called according to his purpose" (Romans 8:28). In order to fully accept our circumstances and gain victory over each discouragement, we must always believe that God is greater than our circumstances.

> *There is no problem too big for God.*

There is no problem too big for God. When we become too problem-conscious, we cease to be Christ-conscious. When we feel overwhelmed by our problems, we are actually doubting the purpose and character of God. Our discouragement and frustration illustrate our belief that God has failed us. In reality, He is always working *for* us (Romans 8:31).

Even the greatest of human tragedies can accomplish invaluable good when we view them in the light of eternity. Our shortsighted temporal viewpoint often blinds us to God's great purposes. The death of Jesus Christ seemed to be a mistake until His resurrection. Death is never a tragedy for the child of God. The Bible tells us, "Precious in the sight of the LORD is the death of his saints" (Psalm 116:15).

Several years ago, at the funeral of a dear godly woman who had died after many years of physical suffering, many people questioned God's wisdom in allowing such a good woman to suffer so much. Through all her suffering, her confidence in God's love had never wavered. At her funeral, the minister read the text, "I consider that our present sufferings are not worth comparing with the glory that will be revealed in us" (Romans 8:18).

As the years rolled by, God used her unwavering testimony to impress upon her children and grandchildren the importance of devotion to Christ. Each time one of them was tempted to turn away from the will of God, he was drawn back by the remembrance of her life and testimony. In a very real sense, though she was dead, she still spoke to them.

Why Do Christians Suffer?

Sometimes suffering is the consequence of sinful disobedience. Sometimes we suffer because we deserve to suffer for our wrong actions. However, this is only one cause of suffering. While Acts 5:3-11 and 1 Corinthians 11:28-31 make it clear that believers may suffer for wrongdoing, the Bible also emphatically states that not all suffering is the result of sin. Job suffered greatly not because of sin, but as a lesson to his friends and to Satan!

The apostle Paul was severely beaten, stoned, and shipwrecked for the cause of the gospel. Throughout church history, many great saints of God have suffered persecution so that the church might grow. Missionaries have given their very lives to bring the gospel to the remote regions of the earth. It is quite obvious that all suffering is not an act of judgment against sin. There are many "causes" of suffering, but all of them are under the control of God. Remember, Satan could not touch Job without God's permission (Job 1:12; 2:6).

Suffering has many purposes:

Cause of Suffering	Purpose of Suffering	Scripture
Sin	To warn us of the consequences of sin	1 Corinthians 11:28-31
Conformity	To conform us in our weakness to Christ's image (His personality)	Romans 12:1-2; 1 Peter 4:12-13
Commitment	To develop deep spiritual qualities in our lives through perseverance	Romans 5:3
Compassion	To enable us to identify with and help others	2 Corinthians 1:4
Encouragement	To testify to those whose faith is weak	2 Corinthians 1:6
Evangelism	To convince the unsaved that God's grace is real	2 Corinthians 4:11; 2 Corinthians 6:3-5

God's Sovereign Purposes

As human beings, we tend to view every circumstance of life from a selfish and temporal vantage point. Our heavenly Father, however, operates from a divine eternal perspective. He sees the consequences of a given event far into the future.

We have all heard stories of the miraculous deliverance of believers from danger. Yet we must not forget those who were not delivered. Millions have suffered death for the cause of Christ over the centuries. Why does God spare some and not others?

Our final answer must lie in God's sovereign purposes. No one deliberately chooses to suffer. We cannot understand the timing and purpose of God adequately to ask to suffer at our convenience. Yet God permits suffering to come into our lives just when we need it most. He reminds us, "Everyone who wants to live a godly life in Christ Jesus will be persecuted" (2 Timothy 3:12). And Paul prayed that the Corinthian church would learn how to suffer: "Our hope for you is firm, because we know that just as you share in our sufferings, so also you share in our comfort" (2 Corinthians 1:7).

God's Sufficient Grace

The apostle Paul had a problem. In 2 Corinthians 12:7-9, he says: "...there was given me a thorn in my flesh....Three times I pleaded with the Lord to take it away from me. But he said unto me, 'My grace is sufficient for you, for my power is made perfect in weakness.'" In Paul's case, God chose to glorify Himself by leaving the affliction, not by removing it.

We all praise God for His miraculous healing of certain family members and friends. But we also need to be aware of those whom God did not heal, some of whom have gone on to heaven. In either case, whether in life or death, God has been glorified. Confronted with pain or tragedy, we must ever turn our faces heavenward and receive God's all-sufficient grace. For the Christian, life is never lost—rather, it is invested in eternity.

Dealing with Adversity

Whenever adversity comes into the life of the Christian, it comes with one of three purposes:

- Temptations—to bring you down (from Satan)
- Tests—to bring you through (from the world)
- Tribulations—to bring you up (from God)

Any adversity that comes into our lives is one of these three. Satan, of course, wants to destroy us and blot out our Christian testimony. Tests and trials, on the other hand, are inevitable consequences of a fallen world. Every day, Christians and non-Christians alike undergo tests of endurance and trials of patience, but only the Christian can rest assured that trials and calamities are God's tool to perfect the character of His children. Some of our problems are initiated by the Lord. These are intended for the development of specific character qualities of Christlikeness and holiness within us, which could not be accomplished by other means. The chart on page 105 compares and contrasts these three difference sources of adversity and suffering.

Eliminate Misconceptions About Suffering.

Misconception 1: When you have problems, it means you are not spiritual. An examination of the Bible quickly reveals that God's closest friends often have the hardest times. Adversity is often God's tool to perfect the believer's character.

Misconception 2: Reading the Bible will automatically solve all your problems. To read the Word, or hear it preached, is not the same as to *obey* the Word. Prayer and perseverance are needed to make the Word come alive in our lives. Here we need the Spirit's work as we read and ponder the Scriptures.

Misconception 3: The answers to all of the problems you will face are explicitly found in the Bible. The Bible is God's inerrant Word, but it has little to say about changing spark plugs or

Category	Source	Affliction	References	Purpose
Temptation	Satan	*Peirasmos,* an intentional event designed to overcome or destroy	1 Corinthians 10:13	To *hinder* the believer's fellowship with God
Tribulations	The world	*Thlipis, a* pressure surrounding the individual *Pathema,* a pressure arising within us. *Kakoucheo,* a pressure directed at us from without	1 Peter 4:12 1 Peter 1:7	To *improve* the believer's ability to withstand setbacks and overcome obstacles
Tests	God	*Purosis,* trial by fire	2 Thessalonians 1:4, 2 Corinthians 1:5; Hebrews 13:3	To *inbuild* more of the character of Christ within the believer

finding your way through downtown Chicago. The Bible focuses on the larger issues of life—man's character and obligations. Tackle these issues, and you will find yourself better able to handle the smaller problems.

Misconception 4. Because you are a Christian, you will not have any problems. This may seem like a ridiculous statement, but, unfortunately, it is the unspoken expectation of many Christians. Christ says in John 10:10, "I have come that they might have life, and have it to the full." He is not implying that God issues an invincible suit of armor to each new Christian at the time of conversion. He is promising abundance in life, sometimes through adversity and sometimes through enjoyment, but always with the manifest purpose of conforming our character to that of Jesus Christ. The Bible tells us that the rains fall both on the good men and the evil men of this world, and so, too, the problems of being human befall Christians as well as non-Christians.

Surrender to a Plan of Action

Expand your lines of communication. We all have a certain level of communication with God. During times of adversity, we need to increase the intensity of our communication with Him through intensified Bible study, Scripture memory, meditation, and prayer.

Limit your vulnerability. A time of adversity is probably not a time to take on more responsibilities. Use that time to consolidate your position spiritually. Try to discern God's will for you.

Limit exaggeration and overstatement. Taking office amid the Great Depression, President Roosevelt declared, "The only thing we have to fear is fear itself." Oftentimes Christians panic during times of trouble and make hasty decisions. God tells us in His Word to "be still and know that I am God." Stop, look, and pray is sound advice. In times of trouble, keep your head.

Watch what you say. There is little to be gained by spreading your problem to everyone in your church, your neighborhood, and your community. It is more common for God to work in the quiet of your own heart, in conjunction with the prayers of a few trusted Christians. Do not share too much, too soon, with too many people—let God work discreetly.

Seek wise counsel. The Bible, especially the book of Proverbs, urges the Christian to seek counsel from godly men and women. The same Holy Spirit dwells in all Christians, and the wisdom brought to you by a brother or sister in Christ may well come from Him. But choose your counselors wisely. Consider their lives: Do they know the Lord? Are they walking with Him?

Be teachable. Christians suffer needlessly when they refuse to learn the first time. Scripture teaches that God opposes the proud and obstinate. Learn from the circumstances God puts you in. Don't put yourself in the position of needing to learn the same lesson over and over.

Trust God's timing. God seldom hurries. The children of Israel waited 400 years before God sent them a deliverer. We too must likewise be prepared to wait. God will work His purposes through our lives to our ultimate good. The Bible reminds us, "Being confident of this . . . he who began a good work in you will carry it on to completion" (Philippians 1:6).

The old saying, "God isn't finished with me yet" still applies. We are not what we will be. We may not be what we should be. But, thank God, we are not what we were when God found us. He is still in the process of shaping our lives to make us like Christ.

> *D*on't give up on God while you are in the middle of your struggle. . . . He will see you through just when you need Him most.

While we are in the process of suffering we may not always understand God's purpose in it. A friend of mine went through a terrible battle with cancer several years ago. He said, "When people asked me what God was teaching me, I used to think, *I don't know—I'm just trying to survive!*"

Hope Makes All the Difference

Don't give up on God while you are in the middle of your struggle. Sometimes it is only later, after the suffering has subsided, that we ever really understand what it was all about.

"I can look back now," my friend says, "and clearly see that God was at work in the whole ordeal. But it wasn't always obvious while it was going on. Sometimes the pain was so great all I could do was hang on and hope."

Hope! Sometimes that's all we need to get us through the crisis. Hope will keep you from giving up on God—even when you've given up on yourself. Hang on—He is right there. He will see you through just when you need Him most.

CHAPTER EIGHT

FINDING INNER PEACE
AND STRENGTH

—⧖—

J ean lowered her head and looked down at the floor as
she talked with Linda.

"I just feel so empty inside," Jean said. "My whole
world seems to be coming apart and I feel helpless to do anything about it."

"Can I help?" Linda asked.

"I don't know if anyone can help me," Jean confessed as tears
filled her eyes.

Struggling with Doubt

Insecure is the word we use to describe when we're feeling
unsure of ourselves and our circumstances. If you were standing
on a frozen lake and suddenly heard the ice crack, you would
become very insecure! You might not know whether to run,
panic, pray, or yell for help, but you would definitely feel insecure. Insecure people often find themselves running around in
total panic and confusion, or immobilized by their fears.

Some people feel insecure because they have judged themselves to be inadequate. They sense that they are inferior to others in some way. If we fall into the trap of comparing ourselves to others, we will almost always come up short. We can always find someone bigger, stronger, smarter, or prettier than ourself.

Insecurity and Self-image

Self-image reflects the value we put on ourselves. A poor self-image (based on insecurity and a sense of inferiority) will affect our attitudes toward ourselves, family, friends, and God. Insecurity can make us do several things that only compound our problems:

- Fear the will of God
- Resist authority
- Use wrong methods to gain acceptance
- Be preoccupied with the way we look
- Daydream about being someone else

The apostle Paul warns us not to measure ourselves against others (2 Corinthians 10:12). The results are always damaging, because we tend to have an inflated opinion of ourselves and measure with such a small yardstick or because we undervalue ourselves and measure against a standard we cannot reach. We can always find someone brighter or abler than ourselves, and succumb to the temptation to become bitter and blame God for the fact that we don't measure up.

The Bible clearly teaches that each one of us is a uniquely created being. We were intended by God to be what we are—physically, mentally, and spiritually. In Psalm 139:14 David exclaims, "I praise you because I am fearfully and wonderfully made; your works are wonderful, I know that full well." He was rejoicing in God's design for his life. He was not reproaching God for His workmanship. He was accepting God's will for his life—including his physical body.

Accepting God's Design

Each person is uniquely designed by God for a special purpose in life. That design was chosen in eternity past, and established at conception. Psalm 139:15-16 says, "My frame was not hidden from you when I was made in the secret place. . . . Your eyes saw my unformed body."

The term "unformed body" comes from the Hebrew word meaning "embryonic mass." This passage plainly states that God did not leave your conception to chance—He had His hand on you from the very beginning! Those tiny cells had everything they needed to make you what you are now. He chose how your cells would unite in order to determine your physical characteristics. God used them and made them multiply. He had a full-grown person in mind. He had *you* in mind.

> *Each person is uniquely designed by God for a special purpose in life.*

The very members of our body were fashioned (developed) from that original imperfect (undeveloped) substance (embryo). Your arms, legs, hands—yes, even your face—were designated by God from the genetic makeup of your parents. No mere chance made you male or female; it was God's doing. Accept yourself for what you are, and you will be able to accept God's will for your life. All the worry and fretting in the world cannot change the color of a single hair. If you can trust God to save you, then you can trust His plan for your life.

A Proper Understanding

Few issues in the Christian faith are more misunderstood than self-concept or self-image. Scripture teaches on one hand that we must have the capacity to accept ourselves (Matthew 22:39), yet at the same time, the Bible condemns pride or complacency (Galatians 6:3). The proper balance is a self-concept that recognizes that no human being is worthy before God apart from the death, burial, and resurrection of Jesus Christ. Christ's intercessory work on our behalf must be personally accepted in order to receive salvation. Though we are but lumps of clay in God's hand, nevertheless, we can become valuable vessels of service to Him. No one is unusable when Christ is in his life.

From Negative to Positive

Five "Down-casters"

"Down-casters" are the things in our lives that undermine self-esteem and foster a negative self-concept. These five are the most damaging:

1. *Discouraging comments.* Our words and comments can build someone up or tear him down. Even your tone of voice tells people what you really think of them. Cutting comments can wound the spirit of a spouse or child and do irreparable damage. Don't become an "expert" on everyone's weaknesses—instead, focus on their strengths.

As Christians, God accepts us, loves us, and sees enormous potential in our lives. It is neither wise nor productive to spend time with people who only discourage us. Negative people will get you down every chance they get. The Bible warns us, "Bad company corrupts good character" (1 Corinthians 15:33).

2. *Unfair comparisons.* Unreal or unfair comparisons often make us hard on ourselves. Another person may need different intellectual, physical, or artistic skills to function where God has put him. Comparisons only produce one of the following: *pride* or *self-rejection.* With pride, we assume our "sphere of influence" is bigger than it really is. With self-rejection, we conclude our "sphere of influence" is worthless and insignificant. Both attitudes are displeasing to our Lord, who wants us to work and bear fruit where He has put us, finding fulfillment in doing His will.

3. *Negative thinking.* Many times, doubts about our own worth come from past experiences. Some people are in the

habit of slighting themselves and their accomplishments. Such negative conditioning is either "taught" or "caught." In either case, negative thinking about one's self or one's abilities is disastrous. The apostle Paul warned young Timothy to stay clear of such thinking. "Don't let anyone look down on you because you are young, but set an example for the believers" (1 Timothy 4:12).

4. *Academic difficulty.* In this age of computers and rising young technocrats, the pressure to perform intellectually can be fierce. It is true that we ought to work hard and do our best. Such pressure, however, can be damaging to our self-image. It can rob confidence from young people who excel in areas other than academics. Encourage your children to do the best they can with their abilities, and don't push them beyond their natural limits. Don't set unrealistic standards that they can't reach—or even *you* can't reach.

5. *Unreasonable expectations.* The apostle Paul was a man who drove himself to achieve God's best for his life. He described himself as "press[ing] toward the mark" for the prize of fulfilling God's goals for him (Philippians 3:14 KJV). And yet Paul knew each man or woman must work out those goals before the Lord. Lofty or unreasonable expectations only make us feel constricted by ideals we can't reach. Eventually they weaken our own proper self-confidence. We need to wait upon God as we try to set goals for ourselves. We need to avoid unreasonable expectations. We should adopt goals that not only stretch our horizons, but also remain within our reach.

Five "Up-lifters"

Just as the five "down-casters" I just shared always undermine a positive self-concept, the following five "up-lifters" do the opposite. They help build self-esteem.

1. *Accept God's purpose.* The first step entails faith that God has given us the potential for something wonderful. Whatever failures we have undergone, however discouraged

we may be about ourselves, we are still created in God's image. As a youngster once said, "God don't make no junk!"

2. *Know and do God's will.* If you have never accepted Christ as your personal Lord and Savior, start by doing so. Become a member of God's family, than make God's Word your steady diet. The Bible puts it this way: "As newborn babes desire the pure milk of the word, that you may grow thereby" (1 Peter 2:2 NKJV). Going on with the Lord means becoming fruitful. Of course, only the Holy Spirit can pro duce the qualities that God longs to see in our lives. As you grow as a Christian, you will see more and more traces of the Spirit's work—erasing negative impressions and deepening your awareness that you are now a sanctified vessel in God's hand.

3. *Involve yourself in the lives of other people.* Nothing cures self-pity and low self-esteem like a healthy concern for others! Throughout the New Testament, both Christ and His apostles are shown constantly giving themselves to other people. Difficulties or tribulations never stopped them. The night before His crucifixion, Christ prayed for the needs of others. Even amid our troubles, we can do the same.

4. *Work hard and persevere.* In Philippians 4:13, Paul triumphantly declares, "I can do all things through Christ who strengthens me" (NKJV). He did not make this remark lightly. The church in Philippi had known persecution, and the young Christians there had undergone much hardship. At such times, there is no substitute for spiritual grit. Paul knew that God will give us the grace and courage we need to succeed.

5. *Be patient.* Ultimately, God is patient with us. He puts up with our blunders, forgives our sins, and helps us to mature in Christ. The truth is, He wants even more than we do to see us develop a proper self-concept. He wants us to be mature Christians for our own good and for His glory. However long the process, He will never forsake us. We

sometimes tend to run ahead of God; we need to slow down and wait for Him. He knows what He is doing.

In Search of Security

Understanding Security

Security comes from accepting God's will for our lives. It is the untroubled knowledge that an all-wise God intends nothing but good for us. His will is *perfect* in every way (*see* Romans 12:2). Scripture reminds us that, "God demonstrates his own love for us in this: While we were still sinners, Christ died for us" (Romans 5:8). He loves us so much that He gave His Son to die for our sins. He invites us to trust Him as our personal Savior and become His child.

Security comes when we realize that God knows all about us and loves us anyway! We can learn to live above our failures, our inadequacies, our mistakes, and our circumstances because we personally know the God who is greater than our greatest fears. He loves us with a binding commitment that will not let us go. Indeed, the Bible says, "Who shall separate us from the love of Christ? Shall trouble or hardship or persecution or famine or nakedness or danger or sword?" Then it answers the question: "No, in all these things we are more than conquerors through him who loved us" (Romans 8:35,37). God's love is a love that never lets go.

Our personal security does not come from within. The human spirit by itself can never produce it. Rather, it is founded on the indwelling Holy Spirit—the One who "testifies with our spirit that we are God's children" (Romans 8:16). He is God living within every born-again believer. We are sealed by Him to God the Father, and our life is "hid with Christ in God" (Colossians 3:3). When we are secure spiritually and personally in the love of God, insecurity has no claim over our lives. We can face any circumstance of life in the secure confidence that God is there, that He is in control, and that He loves us!

Steps That Lead to Security

1. *Believe that God is good.* The prophet Jeremiah captured the essence of God's unchanging love for His children when he recorded the following words: " 'I know the plans I have for you,' declares the LORD, 'plans to prosper you and not to harm you, plans to give you hope and a future' " (Jeremiah 29:11). Not only does God intend to see us through the roughest times of our lives, but He also intends to bless us in the process.

2. *Accept the fact that we are fully responsible for our own behavior.* Modern humanistic philosophy tends to deny this, putting the blame on heredity, upbringing, or anything else other than one's self. But that's not what we find in the Bible. From Genesis to Revelation, Scripture holds man squarely responsible for what he does. No one can *make* us unhappy, angry, or rebellious. No one can *make* us sin. How we respond to life is our choice alone. We can choose to obey God or disobey.

3. *Believe that God will deliver you through any situation.* There are 66 books in the Bible, and all confirm this promise. As believers, we must take it on faith. "The Lord is near to all who call upon Him, to all who call upon Him in truth. He will fulfill the desire of those who fear Him; He will also hear their cry and will save them" (Psalm 145:18-19 NASB).

Faith is a willingness to trust God in both the warm winds of prosperity and the harsh gales of adversity. Faith is both a rock of stability and a key that opens the door to God's provision in our lives. "Without faith it is impossible to please Him, for he who comes to God must believe that He is, and that He is a rewarder of those who seek Him" (Hebrews 11:6 NASB).

Knowing *who* we are in Christ enables us to accept *what* happens in our lives as part of His plan. Once we are convinced that God loves us, we are ready to trust His will for our lives.

When Jealousy Strikes

Jealousy is an attitude of envy or resentment toward others. Jealous people are usually nervous and irritable. They are constantly at odds with other people. They put down others in order to enhance their own self-esteem. They are often suspicious, obstinate, and evil-tongued. The jealous person resents those who seem to be more successful, and he wishes he had what they have.

The root of jealousy is self-pity. It leads to the assumption that our needs are not being met now and probably never will be. It turns an unfriendly eye on the blessings, possessions, and opportunities of others. Jealousy is the ultimate selfishness! It makes us focus on the externals of life: money, position, prestige, security, success. And it leads to bitterness, hostility, and vengefulness.

Jealousy is self-seeking zeal gone out of control. Because of its selfish nature, it inevitably leads to personal conflicts. The jealous person cannot bear to see people succeed. He refuses to rejoice in the blessings of others. Scripture, by contrast, admonishes us to "rejoice with those who rejoice; and mourn with those who mourn" (Romans 12:15). The jealous person can do neither! Since he refuses to rejoice in the blessings of others, he cannot sympathize in their hurts.

Self-pity Is Self-destructive

Self-pity is the ultimate protest against God's providence. It is the refusal to be content with God's provision for your life. It is a selfishness that demands the "right" to have more, be more, do more. Self-pity will ultimately lead to rebellion and despair. The psalmist David admitted that when he became jealous of the wicked, he nearly stumbled (Psalm 73:2-3).

Self-pity is really an expression of our anger toward God. It is the ultimate cause of depression and suicide. It leads to senseless brooding over the circumstances of life. It fixes our thoughts on the negatives of life and denies the possibility of improvement or change. It finally produces such personal misery that we lose the joy of living. It works like this:

Self-pity ⟶ Anger ⟶ Bitterness ⟶ Depression

When this chain of self-destruction remains unbroken, it will lead to deep despair. Self-pity is being angry that we are not what we want to be. As long as we keep demanding more out of life, we will never be satisfied with what we have. Contentment is one of life's most precious benefits, but the jealous person will never find it. True contentment comes only when we relinquish our rights instead of asserting them.

Envy: The Enemy Within

Jealousy is caused by envy (Greek = *phthonos*, "ill will"), which leads to covetousness. Envy is the quality of never being satisfied. It covets what others have in a selfish attempt to reinforce one's own inadequacies. It seeks only its own welfare; it is deaf and blind to the needs of others. Envy is a driving force of self-destruction. It, too, forms a chain of self-destruction:

Envy ➤ Covetousness ➤ Frustration ➤ Hostility

Envy is anger that we do not have what we want. Envy can eat up our soul until we hate people without reason. The envious person will actually speak out or strike out against others. He thinks that life, and therefore God, has been unfair to him. He wants to get back at God by getting at those He has blessed.

Surrender Your Rights

You will never overcome jealousy until you develop true contentment. The only way to eliminate jealousy is to cut it off at its root of self-pity. Contentment comes only when we surrender our so-called rights to God. As long as we keep insisting that we have a right to a better deal, we will never be content.

Self-pity comes from clinging to what we feel we deserve. It enslaves us to the past, thus preventing us from developing our future potential. Jealousy and its two sisters, envy and bitterness, make life miserable. They are not the solutions to our problems. They are self-centered hurts that keep us from finding real solutions.

1. *Admit your selfishness.* Identify self-pity for what it is—sin! Stop dwelling on your hurts and disappointments; self-pity will not ease your pain or heal your hurting heart. Nor will it give you comfort or contentment. It will only drive you to despair.

2. *Deny yourself.* One of the clearest conditions of discipleship is learning to deny yourself, take up your cross daily, and follow Christ (Luke 9:23). Life is a battle with self. Insist upon victory over every selfish desire. Settle for nothing less.

3. *Surrender your rights.* Stop demanding your rights. Surrender them to God and accept whatever He gives back to you as privileges. Jealousy is not caused by our circumstances but by how we respond to our circumstances. Stop *reacting* to your circumstances, and start *responding* to God's working in your life. He is no fool who gives up what he cannot keep to gain what he cannot lose.

4. *Realize who you are in Christ.* As a child of God, you are a joint heir with Jesus Christ. You have nothing to be jealous of. Why should you envy someone else when you have God living within you? Yours is the heritage of eternal life. Heaven is your destiny! Jealousy is a waste of your time and energy. In Him we are overcomers. We all have one thing in common: We have overcome obstacles to get where we are now. Stop feeling sorry for yourself. You are a child of the King—live like it!

5. *Start helping others.* The best way to forget your own troubles is to help someone else with his. Accept the responsibility of being a blessing to someone else. Stop waiting for others to bless you. Start being a blessing and you will receive a blessing. Develop a positive attitude that realizes your struggles can help you meet the needs of others. Learn to bear someone else's burden (Galatians 6:2) and yours will become lighter. God will give you the grace to overcome envy and jealousy when you learn the secret of Psalm 37:4: "Delight yourself in the LORD; and He will give you the desires of your heart" (NASB).

Loneliness is one of the most painful problems in life. You can be in a crowd and still feel all alone—alone with yourself, your fears, your problems, your needs. Hundreds are bustling around you, but still you feel unwanted, unneeded, unimportant. You think: *Nobody understands . . .* or worse, *Nobody cares!* Without a friend to share your burdens, life itself becomes seemingly futile, meaningless.

Recognizing Our Purpose and Place

The Bible tells us that God was in perfect fellowship with Himself in eternity past (Genesis 1:26). Man was created to have fellowship with God (Genesis 2:7), yet God said: "It is not good that man should be alone . . ." (Genesis 2:18 NKJV). Therefore, God created woman to be a suitable helper or partner for man. They were to live in fellowship with each other and with God. What's more, God also gave us the church, which is designed to help us build up one another.

Position. As believers, our position in God's eyes never varies: "My sheep hear My voice, and I know them, and they follow Me; and I give eternal life to them, and they shall never perish; and no one shall snatch them out of My hand. My Father, who has given them to Me, is greater than all; and no one is able to snatch them out of the Father's hand" (John 10:27-29 NASB).

In Romans 8:35-39, we are told that nothing can separate us from Christ's love. Sometimes, though, a coolness creeps into our relationship with God. We feel distant, isolated from Him. Eventually we wonder, *Perhaps God doesn't love me anymore.* If this is so, then your problem is not one of position (that never varies), but relationship. Ask yourself how things stand between you and the Lord. Is there anything you've tried to keep hidden from Him? Have you sought daily fellowship with Him?

Purpose. All of us desire to have a sense of purpose in life. Many people, especially younger people, go through a time of confusion: They don't know who they are or where they're going. What they really have encountered is a crisis of purpose. Often they declare they can find little meaning to life. They turn to others, asking, "What's the true reason for living?" Quite likely, the apostle Paul went through just such a stage in his younger days before he met Jesus Christ. In Philippians 3:8, however, we see a man ardently pursuing the true goal of his life: "More than that, I count all things to be loss in view of the surpassing value of knowing Christ Jesus my Lord, for whom I have suffered the loss of all things, and count them but rubbish in order that I might gain Christ" (NASB). As God's children, we can be confident that our lives have definite purpose.

People. God has created His children to have fellowship with one another. The body of Christ serves many purposes, and one of the most important is to provide an avenue of support, encouragement, and emotional closeness. These are elements sought by the emotionally starved soul. If you are lonely, you owe it to yourself to step out and seek more contact with other human beings. Whether it is volunteering for a community project, taking an arts-and-crafts class, or joining a fellowship group at the church, interpersonal contact is a potent weapon against loneliness. "Two are better than one because they have a good return for their labor. For if either of them falls, the one will lift up his companion" (Ecclesiastes 4:9-10 NASB).

Pleasure. One of the most common causes of loneliness is self-neglect—that is, neglecting our own soul's need for laughter and enjoyment. The Bible speaks often of the importance of laughter; loneliness and discouragement are seen as enemies of God's regenerative work within His people. Proverbs 13:12 describes this need for enjoyment: "Hope deferred makes the heart sick, but desire fulfilled is a tree of life." Legitimate fun nourishes the soul; get out there and find some things you really enjoy doing. Do them regularly, and take a friend along if you can.

Pause. One little-known but very common cause of loneliness in the hectic fast-paced world we live in comes, believe it or not, from avoiding one's own company. Christ understood this well. At intervals, He withdrew to solitary places to reexamine His life and commune with God. Matthew 14:23 says, "After He had sent the multitudes away, He went up to the mountain by Himself to pray; and when it was evening, He was there alone" (Matthew 14:23 NASB).

For a Christian, times set aside for meditation and prayer are really indispensable. There is a certain nourishment the soul requires that is available only in those quiet times of self-reflection and intimacy, which the Christian enjoys with God through the intercessory work of the Holy Spirit. One of the shortcomings of the modern-day church is its lack of emphasis on personal worship and communion with God in the secret closets of our life. When this time of personal intimacy with God is in short supply, one of the symptoms the soul may manifest is an emotional sense of loneliness. The cure is to take a few hours during the next week for some real quality time in prayer and meditation with the Lord.

A Powerful Promise

Loneliness is a mental attitude. If we are living in fellowship with God, we are never really alone. He has promised never to leave us or forsake us (Hebrews 13:5). Just before His Ascension, Jesus declared, "Surely I am with you always, to the very end of the age" (Matthew 28:20). This promise climaxes Jesus' Great Commission. He has sent us out to preach the gospel to the entire world in the assurance of His continuing presence.

> Loneliness is a mental attitude. If we are living in fellowship with God, we are never really alone.

Over the centuries, that promise has sustained many a beleaguered saint. We never really face the problems of life alone because Christ lives in us. He is ever present in the soul of the believer. Loneliness comes only when we lose sight of that truth. Christ promised that He would send the Comforter, the Spirit of truth, the Holy Spirit (John 14:16-18,26). Through the Spirit, we have peace and reassurance that Christ lives within us. A lonely Christian, therefore, is one who has forgotten who he is. He has forgotten that he is a child of the King, and instead begins to live like an outcast. He has set down his spiritual armor (Ephesians 6:10-18) and is wide open to attack. Forgetting his

Lord's victory, he is already preparing for defeat. He is living as though God were dead!

Loneliness is a self-inflicted bitterness. It is the belief that God is not near and does not care about us. What really complicates the problem is that we *know* such thoughts are not true! We know in our heart that we are not alone; we are indwelt by the Spirit of God. We are "partakers of the divine nature"(2 Peter 1:4). Our life is co-eternal with the life of God! When we *feel* alone, it is because we are distracting ourselves from the source of all meaning and purpose in life—God . . . our Creator, Sustainer, and Companion.

No, Never Alone!

As Christians, we are never really alone. Christ is always present in our lives through His indwelling Spirit. We can end up *feeling* alone when we see ourselves as victims of circumstance rather than victorious children of the living God.

Loneliness comes when we fail to live in personal fellowship with Christ on a daily basis. If He is really alive and risen from the dead, why should we ever feel alone? Because a boyfriend dropped you? Because your wife died? Because a close friend moved away? Because of a lost job? No. While there will be pain and we will miss what was in our life before, we will never feel alone because God lives within us!

We are joint heirs of Jesus Christ, who lives within us. We share in all that He is, all that He has. He has given us His righteousness and seated us with Him on His eternal throne! He has made you a child of God with an inheritance in heaven! He has done for you everything you could never have done for yourself!

God's continual daily presence in us will sustain us through all the hard times of life. We are not out on the road of life pushing, shoving, and struggling to succeed all by ourself. The Christian life is far more than a struggle to survive; it is a dynamic and exciting daily personal encounter with the living God!

God Is There!

Even when we have sinned against God, we are not permanently cut off from Him. In the face of his own sin, David cried, "Against you, you only, have I sinned" (Psalm 51:4). Even in his failure, David was still painfully aware of God's presence. In another place, he asks, "Where can I go from your Spirit? Where can I flee from your presence? If I go up to the heavens, you are there; if I make my bed in the depths, you are there. If I rise on the wings of the dawn, if I settle on the far side of the sea, even there your hand will guide me, your right hand will hold me fast" (Psalm 139:7-10). God is everywhere, omnipresent. Thus, even in the depth of his worst sin, David stood in God's presence. Even in hell, there is a knowledge of the reality of the person of God.

Loneliness—that feeling of hopelessness and despair—is real. It has engulfed millions. Yet for the Christian, there is no valid reason for feeling lonely. Why?

- God is always there.
- Jesus promised never to leave nor forsake us.
- We are indwelt by the Holy Spirit of God.
- We live in fellowship with God.
- We are not cut off from God's purposes.
  We *are* His purposes!

The Father sent Christ to redeem us. Jesus has commissioned us to take His gospel to the entire world. We are not struggling to find a purpose in life; we know what that purpose is. We just need to go and do it! Start sharing the message, and you will never be lonely. Remember the Great Commission: "Go and make disciples of all nations.... And surely I am with you always, to the very end of the age" (Matthew 28:19-20).

You have a huge task ahead of you; there's no time for self-pity. There is a world to be won to Christ and you play a vital role in getting it done. Get your eyes off yourself and focus on the task. There is enough for all of us to do to keep us busy for a lifetime!

CHAPTER NINE

GETTING DIRECTION FOR YOUR LIFE

—⟋⟍—

Tom Jackson was a very successful corporate vice-president. He had a great job, a wonderful family, and a fabulous house. He looked like the epitome of success. But inside, he was a bundle of nerves.

"My life is so complicated," he admitted, "that I'm worried all the time that it is going to fly apart at any moment. I want help, but I don't know where to turn."

"Let's try turning to the Bible," I suggested. "You just might find your answer in God's Word."

I could see the strain on Tom's face despite his apparent success. His inner turmoil was more than he could bear. He thought he was alone, but he wasn't.

Worry is practically an epidemic in our affluent society. The medical word for worry is *anxiety*, and every year Americans spend millions of dollars on tranquilizers and nerve relaxers in an attempt to conquer anxiety. Christians get especially frustrated over worry because they know they are not supposed to worry. So they worry about worrying!

Worry is anxiety over circumstances beyond our control. The worrier wants everything to go according to his own plans, and becomes anxious when they don't. Ultimately, worry stems from selfishness and an inability to trust the sovereignty of God: "All things work together for good to those who love God, to them who are the called according to his purpose" (Romans 8:28 NKJV).

The Bible clearly teaches us not to worry; In Philippians 4:6 we read, "Do not be anxious about anything." The Authorized Version says: "Be careful for nothing," meaning, "full of care" (or worry). Sometimes we pray that our worries will go away, but often they don't. How can we deal with the problem of worry?

An Important Distinction

First, we should clarify the distinction between worry and fear. Fear is a natural and healthy response to danger. Fear of pain keeps children from touching a hot stove; fear of falling makes an adult hang on when fixing the roof. For our own protection, God gave us a capacity to be afraid.

Worry, on the other hand, is formless. Nothing concrete brings on the dread of worry. For the most part, we should respond to our fears but cast a critical eye on worry and anxiety. The following chart compares the two:

Fear	Anxiety
1. Comes and goes quickly.	1. Lingers. If anything, it gets worse with time.
2. Usually triggered by a clear-cut threat from without.	2. Usually originates within ourselves. Often we cannot tell what caused it.
3. Specific.	3. Vague, ill-defined.
4. Sharpens the senses. We feel alert, quick to respond.	4. Paralyzing. We dither and hesitate.
5. We focus on the danger from without.	5. The feeling itself is dominant. We grope at random, unfocused.
6. Free of inner conflict.	6. Often generates inner conflict. Our thinking is jerky, indecisive.
7. Goes away when the threat is averted.	7. Causes erratic, disturbed behavior. Lingers even when things seem to get better.

Overcoming Worry

Philippians 4:4-9 gives us five specific steps for conquering the problem of worry. We must follow all five, which are in the form of commands in the original Greek text.

1. *"Rejoice in the Lord always"* (verse 4). Christ is the Lord of circumstances as well as our lives. Nothing can possibly happen that God cannot turn to our benefit. The command to rejoice is based on the fact that our rejoicing is *in* the Lord. True joy is not dependent upon our circumstances, but upon our confidence that God is in control of those circumstances.

2. *"Let your gentleness be evident to all"* (verse 5). The word "gentleness" means reasonable, temperate, or appropriate and implies yieldedness to God. We ought to live a moderate lifestyle because we are yielded to the control of the Holy Spirit. The degree of our inward yieldedness will determine the degree of outward moderation. Yielding to the Lordship of Christ brings comfort in place of conflict. Many Christians worry because they are not presently yielding control of their lives to the authority of Christ. They know Him as Savior and have acknowledged His Lordship, but in their moment of anxiety, they are not consciously trusting in and yielding to His authority.

3. *"Do not worry — pray!"* (verses 6-7). The third step is the most difficult of all, because it sounds so simple: Don't worry—pray! "But I've *tried* that," people often say. Now, there are only two possibilities: Either they have genuinely sought God in prayer and the Bible is untrue, or the Bible remains true but something was lacking in their prayer.

There can be no doubt that the biblical antidote for worry is prayer: "In everything, by prayer and petition, with thanksgiving, present your requests to God. And the peace of God . . . will guard your hearts and your minds in Christ Jesus" (verses 6-7). Prayer includes worship and praise and the petition of requests. It must be rendered in everything (all of life's circumstances).

Having really prayed, the believer must have the confidence that his needs have been made known to God. Worry denies the reality of prayer. Worriers do not really pray; they may utter their anxieties and frustrations before God, but they do not really pray in faith with thanksgiving because they are not at peace with God.

4. *Learn to think right* (verse 8). Wrong thinking is the real cause of worry. Notice that the text does not stop by telling us not to worry, but goes on to tell us how to replace worry with right thinking. We are commanded to think on things that are true, honest, just, pure, lovely, admirable, virtuous, and praiseworthy. While it is true that the power of positive thinking has been overemphasized by some, it is also true that we need to keep our minds on that which is true and right rather than that which is imagined or hasn't happened yet. Right thinking is the basis of right living.

There are five different ways people usually deal with their fear:

Curse the presence of fear and anxiety. This may appear to help in the short run, but eventually produces anger and resentment toward God.

Nurse the fear. This will produce loads of self-pity. It will also lead the person to blame someone else for the problem.

Rehearse the fear and anxiety. This will cause the person to actually cling to his worries and anxiety in an unconscious attempt to manipulate others or gather subtle sympathy from them.

Disperse the fear and worry. This causes "dumping" of problems on others or the taking out of frustrations on others, which can lead to self-denial and self-deception concerning the real causes of the problems.

Reverse the fear and anxiety patterns in the mind. A person can choose to see his problems as *projects* God can use in working out His eventual good. For each disability a person fears he has, God has a matching ability that He will use on their behalf.

There are always hidden possibilities in every circumstance when a person is trusting in God and refuses to quit. Living by faith and expecting God's blessings in spite of the problems will tap His provision in the situation.

Worry comes from dwelling on ourselves and our problems instead of God and His solutions. We need to be Christ-centered, not problem-centered. We need to teach ourselves to meditate on wholesome things. Replace negative anxieties with positive truths—don't surrender control of your life to a problem. Give it over to the Holy Spirit, who can solve the problem.

> *W*orry comes from dwelling on ourselves and our problems instead of God and His solutions.

5. *Learn to live right* (verse 9). Verse 9 tells us that what we have learned, and received, and heard, and seen by example, we must now *do*—that is, practice (Greek present tense, with continuing action). *Do* the truth, and you will conquer worry. Think and act like a Christian with an unshakable trust in Christ's absolute Lordship. Only then can you rejoice in all things, live a yielded life, pray with faith, and think wholesome thoughts.

Spiritual maturity is the antidote to worry (spiritual bondage). But no Christian matures overnight. Don't be discouraged if you are not yet what you can and want to be in Christ. Keep on practicing the Christian lifestyle. As you mature, true Christian conduct will become more and more the pattern of your life. You will find yourself trusting God more and worrying less.

Finances: A Key Cause of Worry

One of the greatest causes of worry for most adults is financial pressure. Our finances are a reflection of our lives; disciplined people usually are disciplined about their finances, while reckless people tend to be reckless with their money.

The key for most of us is finding a balance that works in the area of finances. Nothing is more challenging to a marriage than financial problems. Excessive debt leads to *financial bondage*. When this occurs, we make almost all of our decisions in light of our financial problems.

"I can't tithe to my church," a prominent businessman once told me. "My finances are a mess and we can barely make it as it is," he added.

But the truth was that he was living way beyond the level of his income. He had a $500,000 house, a $5,000-per-month mortgage, four automobiles, two boats, and enormous credit card debts.

"I've prayed for God's help," he insisted, "but I don't think even God could help me now."

"God won't help you," I replied, "until you get your finances in proper biblical order. Do you think that you can live as extravagantly as you do and stand before God one day and tell Him you couldn't afford to tithe? The truth is, you cannot afford *not* to tithe!"

The opposite of financial bondage is *financial freedom*. You don't have to be wealthy to be financially free. You just have to be out of debt. What's more, simplifying your lifestyle may actually improve the *quality* of your life. Eliminating excessive debt eliminates excessive pressure—like heart attacks and nervous breakdowns.

Jesus said, "You cannot serve both God and Money" (Matthew 6:24). The key to Jesus' warning about money is found in the word "serve" (Greek, *douleuo*)—as in service rendered by a slave. His point is clear in the original Greek: One cannot be God's slave and, at the same time, the slave of money.

Money itself is *not* the root of all evil—the *love* of money is the root of all evil (1 Timothy 6:10). Man's unbounded greed often proves his undoing. Millions are corrupted by the desire for things. Yet more believers attribute their financial decisions to "God's leading" than any other matter. When the bottom falls out, they are shocked, bitter, and disillusioned, asking, "How could God let this happen to me?"

A Biblical View of Wealth

Being a Christian does not exempt us from God's laws regarding finances. The Bible clearly teaches that money is God's gift entrusted to faithful stewards (Psalm 8:6; Luke 16:11; 2 Corinthians 8:15). This demands unswerving integrity in every area of our personal and business lives. True financial principles are never at odds with true spiritual ones. Christian ethics hold us strictly accountable for what we do with our money.

Our individual plans and commitments cannot contradict our uniqueness as Christians. We are *in* the world, but we are not *of* the world (John 17:14-16). Money is simply a tool in spreading the gospel (Luke 16:9-13). As such, it is temporary—a thing of this world. Things pass away. Only God, His Word, and His children will remain forever.

For the Christian, wealth can be used in God's service. With it, we can build hospitals and churches, feed the poor, or spread the gospel. Then, too, it can be wasted on self-indulgent living, frivolous activities, and sinful habits. The Bible warns that those who pursue money as an end in itself will die frustrated and unhappy. Such people never understand *why* they have money. When wealth is not used to God's glory, it corrupts its owner.

God has entrusted this world and its resources to mankind. The Bible affirms God's blessing of wealth on men like Abraham, Job, and Solomon. The New Testament speaks of wealthy Christians in the early church, such as Joseph of Arimathaea. At the same time, the apostle Paul observed among the early Christians "not many were influential; not many were of noble birth" (1 Corinthians 1:26). The Bible condemns neither rich nor poor. But it reminds us that God is the Lord of all.

Scripture often speaks positively about buying and selling, the legitimacy of the marketplace, and the right of free individuals to own property. The very land of Israel was God's gift to His people (Joshua 13:7; 21:43). The laws of economics are based upon the Judeo-Christian principles of Scripture. In all Jesus' parables about landowners, He never spoke against the concept of private enterprise. What Jesus condemned was the misuse of wealth.

Wealth is seen as God's blessing (Proverbs 10:22), but the oppression of the poor by the wealthy is clearly condemned (Proverbs 22:22-23). At the same time, Scripture teaches that poverty does not necessarily reflect God's judgment: "Better is a poor man whose walk is blameless," declares Proverbs 19:1. The idea here is obvious: It is better to be poor, honest, and happy than to be rich, guilty, and miserable. God's law commands fair treatment for all men: "Do not pervert justice; do not show partiality to the poor or favoritism to the great, but judge your neighbor fairly" (Leviticus 19:15-16).

Happiness and Money

Money, we are often told, cannot buy happiness. Yet millions expend their lives in the hope that it will. Their lives become an unending quest for the unattainable. What's more, wealth itself is only temporary (Psalm 49:10-12). As we learned from Job, fortunes can vanish overnight.

The real problem with trying to buy happiness is that it's just not for sale! God never made us to be satisfied with material things. Only by living above the material can we ever learn to use it properly. God's aim in giving is not hoarding, but sharing.

The Bible admonishes us to develop the *grace of giving* (2 Corinthians 8:1-7). The churches of Macedonia are cited by the apostle Paul as an example of joyful giving out of deep poverty. It is not *getting* that brings happiness, but *giving*. The apostle also notes that the Macedonian Christians first gave themselves to the Lord and *then* gave of their wealth. The totally committed Christian is one who knows the joy of giving. He is truly a cheerful giver (2 Corinthians 9:7).

Many people are in financial trouble because they have never learned to give. They are obsessed with getting. They have missed the whole purpose of stewardship and discipleship in the area of finances. They love to talk of wealth and success as blessings from God, but they know little of the grace of giving. They want more as added proof of His favor. They never think of themselves as conduits of His grace to others.

Money and Distorted Values

Our attitude toward money and possessions reflects our values. If you value yourself on the basis of what you have, you will be driven by the desire to succeed. If you think money alone will make you happy, you will never be happy. Joy is a fruit of the Spirit and a gift of God (Galatians 5:22). It is not for sale! The poorest believer may own it in abundance. It is not dependent upon our circumstances because it comes from God. Only when we develop the right value system will we ever understand the proper place of money in our lives.

1. *Money and wealth are temporary.* That which is material is temporal. It will not last forever, and may not even last a lifetime. Only the spiritual is eternal. Therefore, spiritual priorities should always come before material priorities.

2. *Christian stewardship is necessary.* Temporary though it may be, we are commanded to be good stewards of what we possess (Luke 12:16-21). Our money should be managed wisely, invested carefully, spent cautiously, and shared joyfully.

3. *Wealth is to be used to God's glory.* When we learn to use our possessions to promote the gospel and invest in God's work, we begin to understand that God does not give us things as an end in themselves. They are to be used to honor Him (Proverbs 3:9).

Causes of Financial Problems

Financial problems can be traced back to a variety of causes:

1. *Greed.* The desire for more always leaves us dissatisfied with what we have. It tempts us to make unwise or extravagant purchases.

2. *Pride.* Sometimes we are driven by pride to want things we cannot afford because they make us look successful. They build up our image.

3. *Ignorance.* Many people simply cannot manage their money.

4. *Laziness.* Some people are broke because they will not work. Their financial problems are but symptoms of a deeper weakness.

5. *Stinginess.* The Bible clearly teaches that those who don't give don't receive (Luke 6:38).

Symptoms of Financial Bondage

Financial bondage comes when people spend more than they make. It leaves them in bondage to their creditors, forever short of ready cash. The symptoms include:

- Overdue bills
- Financial worries
- Confusion
- Covetousness
- Financial manipulation
- Deceitfulness
- "Get-rich-quick" schemes

Financial conflicts are among the major causes of divorce. Women especially can worry about money; they fret when the bills are not paid, taking out their fears and frustrations on their husbands. Decisions are made hastily, and things go from bad to worse. Financial bondage usually leads to carelessness, impulse buying, speculation, and—worst of all—credit buying. Those who charge the most can usually afford the least, and their debts mount up. Getting out of debt becomes their overriding concern. They have little or no time to develop creative options toward financial growth.

Achieving Financial Freedom

In order to break free from financial bondage, several things are necessary:

1. *Transfer "ownership" of all your possessions to God.* Take your hands off. Recognize God's sovereign Lordship over you, your house, your car—everything. Acknowledge that everything you have, you have in trust.

2. *Start tithing.* As Christians under grace, we should view the law's demand (10 percent) as a bare minimum. Christian giving should be spontaneous and abundant. Tightwads get little from God (*see* 2 Corinthians 9:6-8).

3. *Write a budget.* You will never avoid nonessential purchases until you determine just what you must have in order to pay your bills (house, car, food, heat, lights, phone, and so forth).

4. *Stop all unnecessary purchases.* Stop buying things you cannot afford. Such buying is only plunging you deeper into debt and will jeopardize everything you have. Until you have things under control, eliminate unnecessary expenditures (new clothes, dinners out, expensive habits).

5. *Buy nothing on credit.* Pay cash for everything. Credit cards are convenient, but they plunge undisciplined buyers into ruin. "Get it today," we are told. "Pay for it tomorrow." Too often, "tomorrow" becomes *indefinitely.*

6. *Sell fast-depreciating items.* If you are really in over your head, that new car may have to go. Four more years of high payments means you will owe more on it than it's worth. The same holds true for new furniture.

7. *Develop biblical priorities.* Spend your money on things that produce the greatest long-lasting benefit (like your children's education). Avoid temporary fads that are keeping you broke. Evaluate every purchase from God's perspective. Ask yourself: "How will buying this item help the cause of Christ?"

8. *Establish a working income.* You mustn't spend everything you make. Make allowances for tithing, taxes, fixed expenses, debt retirement, savings, and so forth. Only about 70 percent of your total income should have to go toward actual living expenses.

9. *Learn money management.* In the parable of the talents (Matthew 25:14-29), Jesus condemns the poor money manager. Set proper priorities and learn to plan ahead.

10. *Get out of debt.* It may be a wise decision to contact a capable accountant or investment counselor for some professional help and advice in setting up a workable plan for handling your finances. This can be done confidentially, it is usually relatively inexpensive, and it can really help improve the effectiveness of your money management. You will never be financially free until you pay off your debts. A professional advisor may be able to help you achieve freedom sooner. Remember, your testimony is at stake. God's glory requires you do no less!

God never intended for us to live with such distractions as worry, pressure, and uncertainty. All of these must be resolved if we are going to find His direction for our lives. We can't make good decisions about the future while we are suffering the consequences of bad decisions we have made in the past.

Our lives don't have to be lived in constant turmoil. But crises don't usually solve themselves, either. We have to take the necessary steps of action to deal with them. No matter how tough that challenge may be, God's grace will sustain you. He will guide your steps and transform your life if you will follow His principles.

Your future can become so wonderful that it will obliterate the pain of the past. But it will only become what you allow it to be by dealing with life God's way. Let Him direct your choices, and soon you will find the joy of living that God has always intended for you.

CHAPTER TEN

REACHING OUT
TO OTHERS

—∿∿—

J ohn and Heather just sat in total silence. It was their first major fight, and neither wanted to give in to the other. Finally, he looked at her and said, "I don't have anything to say." Heather made no response. She just stared at the wall.

"I said, I don't have anything to say!" John repeated as if he expected a reply.

Heather finally looked at him and said, "I know. You haven't had anything to say for months! So why start now?"

God built a bridge of communication to us, and we need to learn to build bridges to others. Putting up barriers around us will cut us off from genuine communication. It will leave us lonely and empty. "But, there are risks involved in building bridges," some will say. Yes, but the rewards are worth the risk! No one wants to be hurt, but clamming up will leave us alienated and isolated from the very people God may intend to use to bless our life.

Misunderstanding always comes from poor communication. We judge, condemn, and criticize those people and things that we least understand. Out of our own ignorance, we make a situation worse when God wants us to correct it. Don't be the cause of problems; learn to become part of the solution!

Communication reflects the very nature and character of God Himself. He is the source of all communication. He is the God who reveals Himself to mankind. In eternity past, the triune God (Father, Son, and Holy Spirit) was in perfect communication with Himself (Genesis 1:26). God did not create man because He was lonely, but because He chose to do so. At first the world was a picture of the beauty of that harmony. God was in perfect communication with Himself, His world, and with man. Man was in perfect harmony with nature. He was in love with his wife, and they had perfect communication with each other.

Adam and Eve were created in God's image and endowed with human intelligence. They had the gift of communicating instantly—with God and with each other. Theirs was a unique relationship of total communication based on total honesty—until sin entered and shattered their world. With sin came lying, blaming, anger, hatred, murder, cheating, and so forth. Communication was broken! They hid from the God who loved them (Genesis 3:8). They blamed each other for their sin. And the world has never been the same since.

By our sinful nature, we inhibit communication. We start building *walls* to hide within instead of building *bridges* to reach out to others. We lie, we hate, we steal, we criticize, we condemn. Yet, the very God who made us has taken infinite pains to communicate His love to us. In the Old Testament He gave us His law and He sent His prophets to announce His plans. In the New Testament, He sent His Son from heaven to communicate His love to us. God offers us peace, forgiveness, and reconciliation as an expression of His love for us.

We are all in the process of communicating something. We may be communicating warmth, love, and acceptance, or anger, bitterness, and hostility—all of which originate from our inner feelings. What we need to ask ourselves is whether we are helping or hurting others by *what* we are communicating.

Principles of Effective Communication

In Ephesians 4:25-32, the Bible gives five keys to effective communication:

1. *Stop lying. Start telling the truth.* People lie to each other every day! "How are you doing?" someone asks. "I'm fine," is the usual reply, which is not always true. Sometimes when someone is upset, another will ask, "What's the matter?" "Nothing!" will come the reply. People are oftentimes afraid to tell what's really going on in their life.

Honest communication depends on honest conversation. Telling the truth builds bridges; lying builds barriers. When people see you are not being honest with them, they will stop talking to you. The Bible says: "Each of you must put off falsehood and speak truthfully"(Ephesians 4:25).

2. *Stop hating. Start loving.* The Bible also says, "In your anger do not sin. Do not let the sun go down while you are still angry" (Ephesians 4:26). In this passage we are warned not to stay angry because anger destroys communication. Anger can lead to aggressive or depressive behavior; it can cause us to strike out at others or to put down ourselves. Either way, anger can be destructive, hurting ourselves and others.

When anger comes into your life, deal with it quickly and settle it. Don't let a day pass without getting rid of any anger you might have. No one wants to be around an angry person. Anger drives children away from their parents, and it drives husbands and wives away from each other. It destroys communication and thereby destroys relationships. By contrast, genuine love forgives, restores, and communicates.

3. *Stop stealing. Start giving.* Stealers are takers—selfish by nature. The apostle Paul reminds us that we need to stop stealing and develop the grace of giving (Ephesians 4:28). In marriage, some people are selfish "takers." They never learn to give, and their marriage suffers. Selfish people *destroy* communication; unselfish people *build* communication by building bridges to each other with gifts of kindness.

In each of your interpersonal relationships, ask yourself, "Am I a giver or a taker?" Givers tend to see the worth and importance of other people and therefore are apt to bring out the best in others. Takers, on the other hand, tend to see the world solely from their own standpoint. They provoke others to evade, repress, or deny their innermost feelings. Their marriage partner rarely feels the freedom to be himself or herself.

4. *Stop cutting down. Start building up.* "Do not let any unwholesome talk come out of your mouths, but only what is helpful for building others up. . . . And do not grieve the Holy Spirit of God" (Ephesians 4:29-30). Some people excel at cutting down everything and everybody. This passage warns that such negative communication grieves the Spirit of God! Your mouth is to be an instrument of God's grace, not a fountain of bitterness and cursing. Every time you cut someone down, you destroy communication. You drive people away from God instead of drawing them closer to Him. What we communicate verbally should encourage and strengthen those who hear us.

5. *Stop overreacting. Start acting like a Christian.* The Bible urges us to "get rid of all bitterness, rage and anger, brawling and slander, along with every form of malice. Be kind and compassionate to one another, forgiving each other, just as in Christ God forgave you" (Ephesians 4:31-32).

Here the great apostle warns us not to handle our problems like pagans. Don't blow up; that only makes things worse! Notice the chain reaction described in verse 31: We start with bitterness, which soon leads to rage and anger. That, in turn, leads to brawling (verbal fighting), which leads to slander (literally *blasphemy)*, and finally to malice (a deliberate attempt to do someone bodily injury). Such behavior is not of God. It is a worldly response to problems, not the Christian response. Such overreactions drive people away from us and destroy communication.

One of the most common reasons for people overreacting in situations that require skillful communication is a failure to realize just how complex good communication really is. Effective communication can best be thought of as a circular process, made up of at least six components:

1. What you mean to say.
2. What you actually say.
3. What the other person hears.
4. What the other person thinks he hears.
5. What the other person says about what you say.
6. What you think the other person says about what you said.

From this list, it is evident that communication is a complex process. People prone to overreacting when trying to communicate with others may simply misunderstand or overlook the message conveyed in one or more of these six ways. Don't jump to conclusions; give the other person every opportunity to express himself clearly.

> *T*rue Christian behavior leads to real communication with others.

True Christian behavior leads to real communication with others. We who have been forgiven can really forgive. We can communicate with one another because God has communicated His love to us.

Developing Communication Skills

There are four skills you can use to convey an attitude of helpfulness and openness, thus making it easier for someone to talk about his or her problem. These can be thought of as four *listening skills* that enhance better communication.

1. *Ice breakers.* These are phrases that indicate to the other person your willingness to get involved. Phrases such as, "Do you want to talk about it?" or "We need to discuss this, don't we?" convey your interest to the person. If you make evasive or dismissive remarks the other person will sense your disinterest, making real communication impossible.

2. *Acknowledgment and positive regard.* Positive regard simply means approaching another person with the frame of mind that he or she is worthwhile and fully deserving of your attention and concentration. People know when they are being patronized or talked down to. For good communication to occur, both parties must feel accepted as being worthy participants in an open and free discussion based on honesty and positive regard for each other.

3. *Silent listening.* Silent listening simply assures the other person—through your manner, your facial expression, your eyes, and even your breathing—that you are neither bored nor preoccupied, but are fully intent on hearing and understanding what is being said. Averted eyes, glances at your watch, occasional sighs, fidgety hands—all these subtly tell the person you would rather be doing something else and he is wasting his time talking to you. One of the characteristics of great men throughout history is that they knew the surest mark of respect to be undivided attention.

4. *Active listening.* This refers to the short phrases and interjections we use during the process of communication. They tell the other person, "I understand. I'm interested. Tell me more." Active listening is a difficult skill to learn because many of us are often absorbed in our own thoughts. When others sense that we are forever "in our own world" and would rather not be disturbed, they will shy away from engaging us in meaningful communication. Phrases like, "I see what you mean," "Yes, I see," and "Could you help me understand that a little better?" are a part of effective, active listening. They encourage the other person to continue and deepen quality communication.

A Communication Survey

The following survey was developed to evaluate the quality of communication within a marriage relationship, but it can also apply to any close interpersonal relationship—at work, at church, or between friends. Answer *true* or *false* to each question in the survey:

1._____ It irritates you when your spouse questions your judgment or doesn't readily approve of your solution to a problem.

2._____ You privately think of yourself as more logical and realistic than your spouse.

3._____ You rarely give spontaneous compliments to your spouse, but instead find yourself frequently making comments of a critical nature.

4._____ You tend to be short with your spouse—you never say *please* and *thank you* anymore.

5._____ You and your spouse never sit down to chat, except about specific problems.

6._____ You ask your spouse barbed or leading questions when discussing sensitive issues.

7._____ Often you read the paper or watch TV while "conversing" with your spouse.

8._____ You reply with judgments (good or bad, right or wrong, okay or not okay) when your spouse asks you about things.

9._____ Even casual conversations with your spouse are likely to turn into arguments or disagreements.

10._____ Your spouse would probably agree that you tend to cut other people off before they finish talking.

If you answered *true* to four or more questions, you are probably doing too much talking and not enough listening. Sometimes we need to *shut up* so the other person can *open up!* *What* you say, *how* you say it, and *how long* you take saying it all communicate what you are really trying to say. Make sure everyone else really "hears" what you want to say to them.

Are You an Encourager?

Real communication encourages others to respond positively. It often results when we show a genuine interest in someone else's needs. We communicate best when our attitudes, coversation, facial expressions, and body language all cooperate in saying, "I'm really interested in you!" Most people want the assurance that we are really listening to them. When we listen to them, we influence them to listen to us.

Asking questions is an effective way to encourage people to talk about themselves. It shows that we are interested in their lives, jobs, families, needs, struggles, and problems. Questions also allow people to become more open about themselves. Remember, communication is not a one-way conversation about ourselves. It is a mutually shared experience that brings us closer to one another. Hope, help, and encouragement result when we communicate God's love and grace to others. Watch your tongue and use it to God's glory.

CHAPTER ELEVEN

RISING ABOVE OUR CIRCUMSTANCES

—◊◊◊—

Bob and Sandy appeared to have the typical all-American family. Two kids. Great jobs. Upward mobility. A measure of success. And some financial security. It all looked great—on the surface. Then the bomb dropped. She ran off with his best friend.

"I was so shocked I couldn't begin to deal with it," Bob told me. "I just walked around in complete confusion. I felt totally abandoned!"

Sandy divorced Bob. Eventually, she married Bob's friend, who was in the military. What was worse, they took Bob's two children and got transferred to Iceland. For the next five years, Bob never saw any of them.

By the time Bob had any interaction with the kids, they were already grown. Time and distance had placed a barrier between them. When he did see them, he felt estranged from them. But he couldn't figure out why. He assumed they just didn't want a relationship with him any longer.

It was years later, after the girls married, that Bob finally began to realize what had happened. Not only did he feel abandoned by their mother, but they felt abandoned by him. They never saw him. So they lost contact.

Only as adults did the girls begin to realize that their mother kept them isolated from their father. She didn't want to have to deal with Bob. So she (and the girls) stayed away—deliberately. In the girl's minds, dad just seemed to disappear from their lives.

The real tragedy with divorce is that it hurts so many people. Bob felt abandoned by his wife. The kids felt abandoned by their dad. And Bob felt abandoned by his own children.

Being abandoned, for whatever reason, hurts so deeply that it is difficult to deal with. Anyone who has ever been hurt by rejection, betrayal, or divorce knows the pain of feeling abandoned. Feeling helpless, hopeless, and all alone.

Most of us don't deal with that kind of pain very well. It is easy for hurting people to hurt people. We want revenge. We want to lash out at someone else. Often we become a powder keg of emotions waiting to explode.

Joseph: An Example for Us

That's what makes the biblical story of Joseph so unique. He was the son of Jacob and Rachel. Her firstborn, and Jacob's favorite. The sons Jacob had through Leah were such a disappointment to him that he quickly favored Joseph over the others.

Joseph had the advantage of growing up after his father's spiritual turning point at Bethel. Unlike his half-brothers, who had witnessed Jacob's conniving and manipulative lifestyle, Joseph was raised by a dad whose life had been dramatically transformed by God. So Joseph grew up respecting his father and following his godly example.

Joseph's brothers were another story altogether. They were liars, deceivers, manipulators—and those were some of their better qualities! They had even committed murder. By contrast, Joseph was a "goody-goody" and a "daddy's boy." So it was inevitable that there would be problems between them.

The family eventually left Bethel and migrated south toward Bethlehem (Genesis 35:16-20). En route, Rachel, who was pregnant, delivered her second son, Benjamin. But in the process of giving birth, she died. Jacob was heartbroken over the loss of his favorite wife. And Joseph experienced the first pains of feeling abandoned.

To make up for his mother's loss, Jacob showered Joseph with presents, like his multicolored coat. The problem was that such treatment only caused his half brothers to resent him all the more. And then there were his constant dreams about all of them bowing down to him, which only made matters worse.

The Plot Against Joseph

When Joseph was 17 years old, a crisis occurred that changed his life forever. His ten brothers took the family flocks north to graze them near Shechem. After a while, Jacob asked Joseph to go and check on them and the sheep.

When Joseph arrived in the region, he was told his brothers had moved on to Dothan. So he went looking for them. But when they saw him coming, they resented his intrusion so much that they plotted to kill him.

"Here comes that dreamer!" they shouted. "Come now, let's kill him and throw him into one of these cisterns and say that a ferocious animal devoured him. Then we'll see what comes of his dreams" (Genesis 37:19,20).

Reuben, the eldest, tried to rescue him, but to no avail. Then Judah suggested they sell him to a passing caravan of Arab traders. Good idea! They all agreed. And Joseph was sold into slavery for 20 pieces of silver.

To cover their ill-gotten gain, the brothers tore up the colorful robe and soaked it in goat's blood. When Jacob saw the bloody robe, he assumed Joseph had been eaten by a wild animal. Jacob's grief was so great that he refused to be comforted. He sobbed uncontrollably. "In mourning will I go down to the grave to my son," he insisted.

The real tragedy was that Jacob remained in agony over this deception for 20 years. In the meantime, Joseph had plenty of problems of his own.

From the Pit to the Prison

The Arabs eventually sold Joseph into slavery in Egypt. In the providence of God, he was purchased by an Egyptian official, Potiphar, the captain of Pharaoh's guard. And he was taken to Potiphar's house, where he quickly rose to the position of chief steward and his master's personal attendant.

But it wasn't long before new problems arose. Potiphar's wife took an interest in Joseph. Perhaps she was bored and felt neglected by her busy husband. Or perhaps she was attracted to Joseph's handsome physique. Whatever the reason, she risked telling him how she felt.

> The real test of human character comes when the bottom falls out of our lives.

"Come to bed with me," she suggested.

But Joseph refused. "How then could I do such a wicked thing and sin against God?" he protested (Genesis 39:9).

The biblical account indicates that she kept at him day after day. Most men would have given in to the temptation: *He's gone. There's no one home. We're both adults. Besides, she needs it. Why not? What harm could it do?*

Not Joseph. He stood his ground, refusing her advances day after day. That's where we see what this young man is made of. The depth of his character was impeccable. And his confidence in God was incredible even in this difficult circumstance.

The real test of human character comes when the bottom falls out of our lives. That's when our faith in God is challenged: *Can I still trust after everything that has happened to me? If He really loves me, how can He even let this happen to me? Living for Him just isn't paying off!*

When Joseph continued to refuse his master's wife, she turned on him with a vengeance. First, she threw herself at him. But he ran off, leaving his cloak in her hands. He got into more trouble over his clothes! Angered by Joseph's rejection, she went to her husband and falsely accused Joseph of attempting to seduce her.

Being a slave meant you were very susceptible to an accusation. Joseph had no legal recourse. He was condemned and thrown into the royal dungeon. But even there, Joseph refused to turn against God. He became a model prisoner. In time, he was made the warden's assistant.

From Prison to the Palace

We don't know the exact time line of all the details in Joseph's life. But we do know he was sold by his brothers when he was 17 (Genesis 37:2). And he languished in prison until he was 30 (41:46). Thirteen years passed until his big break came.

Think of all that Joseph had been through:

1. Painful death of his mother.
2. Jealous resentment of his brothers.
3. Betrayal and abandonment by his family.
4. Humiliation of human slavery.
5. False accusation and imprisonment.

Despite all this, he never gave up on God. There was no hint of bitterness or hostility. In every situation, Joseph rose above his circumstances by the power of God.

Genesis 40 records the story of Pharaoh's butler and baker being thrown into the royal dungeon and their personal encounter with Joseph. He interpreted their dreams and begged them to plead his innocence to Pharaoh. Even though the interpretations came true, the butler (cupbearer) forgot about Joseph for two more years. Finally, a crisis occurred when Pharaoh had a troubling dream of his own (Genesis 41:1).

That's when everything changed. The butler told Pharaoh about Joseph's ability to interpret dreams. And the royal decree went forth to release him from prison. He quickly shaved and changed into white linen in order to stand before the king in proper Egyptian attire.

"I have heard it said of you that when you hear a dream you can interpret it," Pharaoh said inquisitively (41:15).

"I cannot do it," Joseph replied, "but God will give Pharaoh the answer he desires" (41:16).

Then Joseph proceeded to interpret Pharaoh's dreams about seven fat cows and seven lean cows as seven years of prosperity, followed by seven years of famine. Not only did Joseph give the monarch a glimpse into the future, but he proceeded to give him some administrative advice as well.

"And now," he suggested, "let Pharaoh look for a discerning and wise man and put him in charge of the land of Egypt" (41:33). Joseph further advised that they store a fifth (20 percent) of the annual harvest during the years of plenty. That would provide ample reserves for the years of famine in the future.

Pharaoh was so taken by Joseph's advice that he appointed him to become the grand vizier of Egypt. He would personally oversee this great administrative task of collecting, storing, and distributing the grain.

"Can we find anyone like this man, one in whom is the spirit of God?" Pharaoh asked. "There is no one so discerning and wise as you," he added. In one of history's dramatic reversals, Joseph went from the prison to the palace instantly. One cannot help but wonder what Potiphar and his wife must have thought!

If Only They Could See Me Now

Everything changed overnight for Joseph. No more restless nights in the dungeon. He was sleeping in the palace. No more ragged clothes. He was dressed in royal robes, riding in the royal chariot. They even gave him an Egyptian name and an Egyptian wife (41:45). He was a big deal. If only his brothers could see him now!

Just as he had predicted, the seven years of plenty came. And they stored up so much grain they couldn't keep up with it all. But then the famine came as well. And Joseph sold the grain to the Egyptians, which increased Pharaoh's wealth all the more.

Eventually people began coming from other countries to buy grain.

Joseph was now 37 years old. It had been 20 years since he had seen his family. But in all those tough times, God had not forgotten him. Neither had He forgotten the promise. In fact, if Joseph hadn't been in Egypt, all might have been lost. God was going to preserve the entire family through Joseph's provision.

The famine was so severe it reached Canaan as well (Genesis 42:1-2). And Jacob sent ten of his sons to Egypt to buy grain, but he kept Benjamin safely at home. When they arrived in Egypt, Joseph immediately recognized his brothers. But they did not recognize him. He looked like an Egyptian, walked like an Egyptian, and talked like an Egyptian. So they naturally thought he was an Egyptian.

"Where do you come from?" he asked them harshly through an interpreter.

"From the land of Canaan," they replied, "to buy food."

"You are spies!" Joseph insisted.

"No!" they replied. "Your servants were twelve brothers, the sons of one man.... The youngest is now with our father, and one is no more," they added lamentably (42:13).

Joseph proceeded to tell them that one of them would have to remain behind as a hostage while the others returned to Canaan to get their younger brother.

"You must bring your youngest brother to me," Joseph insisted, wanting to see his brother.

Then the brothers turned to each other and said, "Surely we are being punished because of our brother." And they proceeded to discuss what they had done to Joseph and how guilty they felt.

All the time, Joseph was listening to every word they were saying. But he never let on that he understood them. Finally, he couldn't take it anymore and he began to weep. So he walked away.

Bad News and More Bad News

Joseph kept Simeon as the hostage. I've often wondered if he was the one who had been most hostile toward him. He certainly paid for it if he was. In the meantime, the other brothers set off for home. Their bags were loaded with grain, and their money was returned as well. But when they got back home without Simeon, Jacob threw a fit!

"You have deprived me of my children. Joseph is no more and Simeon is no more, and now you want to take Benjamin. Everything is against me!" (Genesis 42:36).

Now, on the surface of things, it may well have appeared that everything really was going *against* Jacob. But in reality, God was moving *for* Jacob. He was at work in every circumstance to accomplish His will and purpose in Jacob's life and in his entire family. It was all coming together like a grand masterpiece.

Reluctantly, Jacob finally agreed to let Benjamin return to Egypt with his other sons. It was a risky choice. This was Joseph's full brother. Rachel's other son. Jacob couldn't bear the thought of losing him too. But Judah spoke up and promised to personally guarantee his safety.

"God Almighty grant you mercy," Jacob said. "As for me, if I am bereaved, I am bereaved" (43:14). He had experienced so much pain that he abandoned himself and his family to God.

When they arrived in Egypt, Joseph was anxious to see them. But the sight of Benjamin was more than he could bear. Again, he ran out of the room and sobbed. When he returned, he tried to act tough with them again. But Judah begged him for mercy, even offering to be his personal slave if he would not harm Benjamin.

Judah begged Joseph, telling him what their father had said: "If you take this one from me too and harm comes to him, you will bring my gray head down to the grave in misery" (44:29). "He is so close to the boy, he'll die if we go back without him," Judah explained.

The Truth Comes Out

The grief they were all expressing was more than Joseph could bear. Finally, he burst into tears in front of them and told them who he was.

"I am Joseph! Is my father still living?" he asked.

They were absolutely terrified! All ten of them stood there in stunned silence.

Joseph! The prime minister of Egypt? The grand vizier of the whole land? Second only to Pharaoh? Oh, no!

He's going to kill us! they probably thought.

"Come close to me," he said. "I am your brother Joseph, the one you sold into Egypt! And now, do not be distressed . . . for selling me here, because it was to save lives that God sent me ahead of you . . . to preserve for you a remnant on earth and to save your lives by a great deliverance" (Genesis 45:4-7).

He explained the famine would last for seven whole years. Then he asked them to go home and insist that Jacob and the entire family move to Egypt to keep them alive.

"Tell him God has made me lord of all Egypt. Come quickly. Don't delay," Joseph insisted. Then he loaded them with provisions for the trip home. He sent a caravan of 20 donkeys and carts.

It must have been some meeting when the brothers had to tell their father that they had deceived him all those years.

"Joseph is still alive!" they announced. "In fact, he is ruler of all Egypt" (45:26).

Jacob was so stunned, he could not believe them at first. But as they unravelled their story, he realized it was true. And his spirit revived. Hope sprang anew in those old eyes.

"I'm convinced! My son Joseph is still alive," he shouted. "I will go and see him before I die" (45:28).

What happened next was an incredible sight! They packed up their belongings, took down their tents, rounded up their cattle, and the group of 70 people pulled out of Beersheba, heading toward Egypt. Excitement and anticipation beat in every heart. The men, women, and children, who would become the nation of Israel, were headed to an appointment with destiny.

Jacob wasn't running for his life this time. He was riding in style. His son was the prime minister of Egypt. And he had an appointment with royalty to keep. He was going to meet the

Pharaoh. But more than anything, he was going to see his beloved Joseph again face to face.

When Jacob arrived, Joseph threw his arms around his father and wept a long time. The son presumed dead was alive. Jacob was finally satisfied.

"Now I am ready to die," Jacob said. "I have seen you for myself."

What a great reunion it must have been. Not just of a father and a son, but of a whole family.

All's Well That Ends Well

> God is still in the business of happy endings. He still takes shattered lives and rebuilds them to His glory.

Joseph's family settled in the fertile delta area in Lower (northern) Egypt. There they prospered and multiplied in the years to come. God had reversed the brothers' hostility into blessing. He had overruled their wickedness and made Joseph ruler of Egypt.

Several years later, Jacob died at a good old age. And Joseph had the body embalmed. Then a royal procession carried his mummified remains back to Canaan to the burial place of Abraham and Isaac. Jacob's wanderings were over. He was finally coming home. And what a homecoming it was!

God is still in the business of happy endings. He still takes shattered lives and rebuilds them to His glory. Remember Bob at the beginning of the chapter? God sustained him through the divorce and the separation from his children. He later remarried and committed his life to full-time ministry. Today, he is one of the nation's leading ministers to singles. And his marriage is a model of Christian love and devotion.

You may feel that your life has been shattered by some personal crisis. But God can still turn it all around to His glory. Trust Him! He's already in the process of working it out.

CHAPTER TWELVE

PROBLEMS ARE REALLY OPPORTUNITIES

—∞—

In terms of the ultimate purposes of God, we really don't have any problems; we have opportunities! As we've seen in this book, God allows problems to come into our lives to help us learn to trust Him more. Every time we exercise faith in Him, we are actually growing spiritually. Thus, our problems are really opportunities for spiritual growth. Romans 8:28 promises us that "all things work together for good to those who love God, to those who are the called according to His purpose" (NKJV). Spiritual maturity is learning to view every problem of life as a new opportunity to experience the good purpose of God in our daily lives.

The key to handling any problem is committing it totally to God. When problems come—and they will—we must learn that trusting God is our *first resource*, not our *last resort.*

Our ability and willingness to trust God in every circumstance depends upon our confidence in His goodness and His motives. All uncertainty on our part is ultimately distrust of His basic nature and character. The person defeated by life's problems is ultimately questioning God's integrity. If He really is an all-wise and all-loving God, then we must learn to trust Him and His Word in the face of any problems we may have.

From God's point of view, you don't have any problems—just opportunities! If you will learn to see your problems as opportunities, you will have made the first real step toward learning to trust God to turn those opportunities into full-fledged *blessings* in your life. If you can trust God to save you, then you can trust Him to help you. His will is to give you all good things (Romans 8:32) and to fill your life with joy (John 15:11).

> *From God's point of view, you don't have any problems—just opportunities!*

When the road of life gets rough, God is always there, reaching out to help us. When we learn to trust Him and reach out to Him by faith, we find the path easier to walk. Where once we stumbled, now there is progress. Where once we crawled, now we can run. The prophet Isaiah said, "Those who hope in the LORD will renew their strength. They will soar on wings like eagles; they will run and not grow weary, they will walk and not be faint" (40:31).

Whatever your problems may be, they pale in insignificance in the light of eternity. No matter how great your failures, God's grace is greater still. Lift up your heart and face life head-on. Don't avoid your problems; tackle each one directly, knowing that God will help you through. The tougher the problem, the greater His grace will be.

Remember, no one is up all the time. When we are on top of things, we need to pull up those who are down so that when we are down they can pull us up. That is what the family of God is all about. Each one ministers to the other so that all are helped.

Never give up! The last hill always seems like the toughest. Life is a marathon, not a 100-yard dash. You can't win the race in the first lap. You have to keep running until you're finally home. Pace yourself. Be prepared for the detours and trouble spots.

When they come along, don't give up the race. Remember, when the going gets tough, the tough get going.

God understands your struggle. He designed the trouble spots to strengthen you and to mature you for the final lap. He also knows how much you can take. He will never put more on you than He has put within you to meet the challenge.

May God grant you grace for the journey!

APPENDIX

Biblical Solutions to
Life's Toughest Problems

—∿—

Anger

Biblical Definition:

Greek, *orge,* a natural "impulse" or hostile emotion. Similar to "hatred" (Greek, *ectra*). Anger is the most damaging of all emotions because it can lead to hatred, revenge, and even murder. Anger boils up in the soul and causes us to strike out at others. It is the opposite of *love.*

Biblical References:

"Get rid of all bitterness, rage and anger, brawling and slander, along with every form of malice" (Ephesians 4:31).

"I tell you that anyone who is angry with his brother will be subject to judgment" (Matthew 5:22).

"I tell you: Love your enemies and pray for those who persecute you, that you may be sons of your Father in heaven" (Matthew 5:44).

"Hatred stirs up dissention, but love covers over all wrongs" (Proverbs 10:12).

"A gentle answer turns away wrath, but a harsh word stirs up anger" (Proverbs 15:1).

Bitterness

Biblical Definition:

Greek, *pikria*, "sharp," "piercing hurt," or "bitterness." Bitterness is a deep, harbored hurt that poisons the soul. It eats away the vitality of your spiritual life like a cancer of the soul. It is the opposite of forgiveness.

Biblical References:

"See to it that no one misses the grace of God and that no bitter roots grows up to cause trouble and defile many" (Hebrews 12:15).

"Each heart knows its own bitterness, and no one else can share its joy" (Proverbs 14:10).

"Out of the same mouth come praise and cursing. . . . This should not be" (James 3:10).

"If your brother sins, rebuke him, and if he repents, forgive him" (Luke 17:3).

"Rejoice in the Lord always. Let your gentleness be evident to all" (Philippians 4:4-5).

Conflict

Biblical Definition:

Greek, *eris*, meaning "strife" or "quarrel." Conflict produces division and leads to instability and confusion. When we react negatively to conflict we lose the purpose of it and repeat the problem all over again.

Biblical References:

"Blessed are the peacemakers, for they will be called sons of God" (Matthew 5:9).

"You have heard that it was said, 'Eye for eye, and tooth for tooth.' But I tell you, Do not resist an evil person. . . . Love your enemies and pray for those who persecute you" (Matthew 5:38-39,44).

"Why do you look at the speck of sawdust in your brother's eye and pay no attention to the plank in your own eye?" (Matthew 7:3).

"I appeal to you, brothers . . . that there may be no divisions among you and that you may be perfectly united in mind and thought" (1 Corinthians 1:10).

Death

Biblical Definition:

Greek = *thanatophobia*, which means "fear of death." Human fear of dying is the opposite of trusting God with our temporal lives and our eternal destiny. Death is the great "equalizer" that afflicts the rich and poor alike.

Biblical References:

"The wages of sin is death, but the gift of God is eternal life in Christ Jesus our Lord" (Romans 6:23).

"Man is destined to die once, and after that to face judgment" (Hebrews 9:27).

"Even though I walk through the valley of the shadow of death, I will fear no evil, for you are with me" (Psalm 23:4).

"Jesus said to her, 'I am the resurrection and the life. He who believes in me will live, even though he dies'" (John 11:25).

"For the trumpet will sound, the dead will be raised imperishable, and we will be changed. . . . then the saying that is written will come true: 'Death has been swallowed up in victory'" (1 Corinthians 15:52,54).

Depression

Biblical Definition:

Greek, *exaporeomai*, "to find no way through," to be at a total "loss." The biblical term for depression focuses on the mental frustration of the depressed person. Biblically speaking, depression comes about when a person has exhausted all hope and lapsed into spiritual isolation.

Biblical References:

"When I kept silent,
       my bones wasted away
       through my groaning all day long.
For day and night
       your hand was heavy upon me;
My strength was sapped
       as in the heat of summer" (Psalm 32:3-4).

"Scorn has broken my heart
       and left me helpless;
I looked for sympathy, but there was none,
       for comforters, but I found none" (Psalm 69:20).

"Therefore I despise myself
       and repent in dust and ashes" (Job 42:6).

"Why are you downcast, O my soul?
       Why so disturbed within me?
Put your hope in God,
       for I will yet praise him,
       my Savior and my God" (Psalm 42:11).

"God did not give us a spirit of timidity, but a spirit of power, of love and of self-discipline" (2 Timothy 1:7).

"We are hard pressed on every side, but not crushed; perplexed, but not in despair; persecuted, but not abandoned; struck down, but not destroyed" (2 Corinthians 4:8-9).

"I have learned the secret of being content in any and every situation. . . . I can do everything through him who gives me strength" (Philippians 4:12-13).

Divorce

Biblical Definition:

Greek, *apoluo*, "to loose" or "send away." Similar to *aphienai*, to "release" or "separate." The biblical term refers to the legal separation and dissolution of a marriage. Divorce is a civil act that dissolves the marriage contract. While it is not encouraged, it is permissible under certain circumstances, such as adultery.

Biblical References:

"If a man marries a woman who becomes displeasing to him because he finds out something indecent about her, and he writes her a certificate of divorce, gives it to her and sends her from his house, and if after she leaves his house she becomes the wife of another man, and her second husband . . . writes her a certificate of divorce . . . or if he dies . . . her first husband, who divorced her, is not allowed to marry her again" (Deuteronomy 24:1-4).

"It has been said, 'Anyone who divorces his wife must give her a certificate of divorce.' But I tell you that anyone who divorces his wife, except for marital unfaithfulness, causes her to become an adulteress, and anyone who marries the divorced woman commits adultery" (Matthew 5:31-32).

"'Haven't you read,' [Jesus] replied, 'that at the beginning the Creator made them male and female,' and said, 'for this reason a man will . . . be united to his wife, and the two will become one flesh'? So they are no longer two, but one. Therefore what God has joined together, let man not separate" (Matthew 19:4-6).

"A wife must not separate from her husband. But if she does, she must remain unmarried or else be reconciled to her husband. And a husband must not divorce his wife. . . . If any brother has a wife who is not a believer and he is willing to live with her, she must not divorce him. . . . But if the unbeliever leaves, let him do so. A believing man or woman is not bound in such circumstances" (1 Corinthians 7:10-13,15).

"Are you married? Do not seek a divorce. Are you unmarried? Do not look for a wife. But if you do marry, you have not sinned; and if a virgin marries, she has not sinned" (1 Corinthians 7:27-28).

Failure

Biblical Definition:

Greek, *ekleipo*, "to fail," "give up," or "fall short" the opposite of success. Biblically, failure is never final until you quit trying.

God offers us sufficient grace and strength to overcome our failures and turn our weaknesses into strengths.

Biblical References:

"All have sinned and fall short of the glory of God" (Romans 3:23).

"Jesus continued: 'There was a man who had two sons. . . . the younger son . . . set off for a distant country and there squandered his wealth in wild living. . . . When he came to his senses, he said, " . . . I will set out and go back to my father" . . . But while he was still a long way off, his father saw him and was filled with compassion for him; he ran to his son, threw his arms around him and kissed him'" (Luke 15:11,13,17,20).

"Do not let this Book of the Law depart from your mouth; meditate on it day and night. . . . Then will you be prosperous and successful" (Joshua 1:8).

"If God is for us, who can be against us? . . . Who shall separate us from the love of Christ? . . . No, in all these things we are more than conquerors through him who loved us" (Romans 8:31,35,37).

"I can do everything through him who gives me strength" (Philippians 4:13).

Finances

Biblical Definition:

Greek, *mammonas*, "wealth" or "material possessions." Taken from the name of the Greek god of material wealth. This term is used both positively and negatively in the New Testament in relation to one's attitude toward money, wealth, and prosperity.

Biblical References:

"The love of money is a root of all kinds of evil. Some people, eager for money, have wandered from the faith and pierced themselves with many griefs" (1 Timothy 6:10).

"No one can serve two masters. Either he will hate the one and love the other, or he will be devoted to the one and despise the other. You cannot serve both God and Money" (Matthew 6:24).

"I tell you, use worldly wealth to gain friends for yourselves, so that when it is gone, you will be welcomed into eternal dwellings. . . . So if you have not been trustworthy in handling worldly wealth, who will trust you with true riches?" (Luke 16:9,11).

"Give, and it will be given to you. A good measure, pressed down, shaken together and running over, will be poured into your lap. For with the measure you use, it will be measured to you" (Luke 6:38).

"The blessing of the LORD brings wealth, and he adds no trouble to it" (Proverbs 10:22).

"See that you also excel in this grace of giving. . . . For you know the grace of our Lord Jesus Christ, that though he was rich, yet for your sakes he became poor, so that you through his poverty might become rich" (2 Corinthians 8:7,9).

"Remember this: Whoever sows sparingly will also reap sparingly, and whoever sows generously will also reap generously. . . . For God loves a cheerful giver" (2 Corinthians 9:6-7).

"God will meet all your needs according to his glorious riches in Christ Jesus" (Philippians 4:19).

Guilt

Biblical Definition:

Greek, *hupodikos,* "liable," as in liable to be brought to trial for doing something wrong. Legal guilt is the result of being judged. Personal guilt is the feeling of judgment in one's conscience. Guilt may lead to repentance or it may be suppressed as one hardens his heart against God.

Biblical References:

"The wrath of God is being revealed from heaven against all the godlessness and wickedness of men who suppress the truth by their wickedness . . . so that men are without excuse" (Romans 1:18,20).

"You, therefore, have no excuse, you who pass judgment on someone else, for at whatever point you judge the other, you are condemning yourself" (Romans 2:1).

"There is now no condemnation for those who are in Christ Jesus, because through Christ Jesus the law of the Spirit of life set me free from the law of sin and death" (Romans 8:1-2).

> "Blessed is he
> > whose transgressions are forgiven,
> > whose sins are covered.
> Blessed is the man
> > whose sin the LORD does not count against him
> > and in whose spirit is no deceit.
> When I kept silent,
> > my bones wasted away
> > through my groaning all day long.
> For day and night
> > your hand was heavy upon me. . . .
> Then I acknowledged my sin to you. . . .
> I said, 'I will confess
> > my transgressions to the LORD'—
> And you forgave
> > the guilt of my sin" (Psalm 32:1-5).

"If we confess our sins, he is faithful and just and will forgive us our sins and purify us from all unrighteousness" (1 John 1:9).

Insecurity

Biblical Definition:

Greek, *hettaomai,* to be "less" or "inferior." The opposite of confident or sufficient. Insecurity is caused by fearful uncertainty. Feelings of inferiority are caused by a self-judgment of inadequacy. They are similar and often interrelated—feeling inferior breeds insecurity, and insecurity breeds feelings of inferiority.

Biblical References:

"We do not dare to classify or compare ourselves with some who commend themselves. When they measure themselves by themselves and compare themselves with themselves, they are not wise" (2 Corinthians 10:12).

"If anyone thinks he is something when he is nothing, he deceives himself. Each one should test his own actions. Then he can take pride in himself, without comparing himself to somebody else, for each one should carry his own load" (Galatians 6:3-5).

"You created my inmost being;
    you knit me together in my mother's womb.
I praise you because I am fearfully and wonderfully made;
    your works are wonderful,
I know that full well" (Psalm 139:13-14).

"Being confident of this, that he who began a good work in you will carry it on to completion until the day of Christ Jesus" (Philippians 1:6).

"Don't let anyone look down on you because you are young, but set an example for the believers in speech, in life, in love, in faith and in purity" (1 Timothy 4:12).

"'For I know the plans I have for you,' declares the Lord, 'plans to prosper you and not to harm you, plans to give you hope and a future'" (Jeremiah 29:11).

Loneliness

Biblical Definition:

Greek, *monos,* meaning "single" or "alone." Taken to an extreme, it leads to a sense of separation or alienation from others. It can lead to the feeling that nobody cares about us. Without a close friend to share our burdens, life can become difficult and seem meaningless.

Biblical References:

"The LORD God said, 'It is not good for the man to be alone. I will make a helper suitable for him'" (Genesis 1:18).

"Two are better than one,
        because they have a good return for their work:
If one falls down,
        his friend can help him up" (Ecclesiastes 4:9).

"Be content with what you have, because God has said,
        'Never will I leave you;
                never will I forsake you.'
So we can say with confidence,
        'The Lord is my helper; I will not be afraid.
                What can man do to me?'" (Hebrews 13:5-6).

"Surely I am with you always, to the very end of
        the age" (Matthew 28:20).

"Do not let your hearts be troubled. Trust in God; trust also in me. . . . I am going . . . to prepare a place for you. And if I go and prepare a place for you, I will come back and take you to be with me that you also may be where I am" (John 14:1-3).

"I am convinced that neither death nor life, neither angels or demons, neither the present nor the future, nor any powers . . . will be able to separate us from the love of God that is in Christ Jesus our Lord" (Romans 8:38-39).

Pressure

Biblical Definition:

Greek, *biazomai,* to be "pressed down" or "constrained." In its most extreme forms, pressure can cause us to crack mentally, emotionally, and even spiritually. Under the pressure of Jesus' trial at the high priest's home, Peter cracked and denied the Lord three times (Luke 22:54-62). John Mark turned back on the first missionary journey under the pressure of the great endeavor itself (Acts 15:37-38). The opposite of pressure is patience or endurance (Greek, *hupomenè,* to "hold up under" pressure).

Biblical References:

"Come to me, all you who are weary and burdened, and I will give you rest. Take my yoke upon you . . . and you will find rest for your souls. For my yoke is easy and my burden is light" (Matthew 11:28-30).

"Peace I leave with you; my peace I give you. . . . Do not let your hearts be troubled and do not be afraid" (John 14:27).

"The fruit of the Spirit is love, joy, peace, patience, kindness, goodness, faithfulness, gentleness and self-control" (Galatians 5:22-23).

"Let us then approach the throne of grace with confidence, so that we may receive mercy and find grace to help us in our time of need" (Hebrews 4:16).

"Trust in the LORD with all your heart
      and lean not on your own understanding;
   in all your ways acknowledge him,
      and he will make your paths straight" (Proverbs 3:5-6).

Rejection

Biblical Definition:

Greek, *atheteo,* to "cast aside" or "refuse" as unfit or unworthy. Rejection is the opposite of acceptance. We cannot control who will accept us and who will reject us. But we can be assured that God loves us and accepts us in Christ Jesus. God's acceptance is the basis of our personal security and inner stability.

Biblical References:

"Cast your cares on the LORD
      and he will sustain you;
   he will never let the righteous fall" (Psalm 55:22).

"All that the Father gives me will come to me, and whoever comes to me I will never drive away" (John 6:37).

"The Spirit himself testifies with our spirit that we are God's children. Now if we are children, then we are heirs—heirs of God and co-heirs with Christ" (Romans 8:16-17).

"I am not ashamed, because I know whom I have believed, and am convinced that he is able to guard what I have entrusted to him for that day" (2 Timothy 1:12).

"How great is the love the Father has lavished on us, that we should be called children of God! And that is what we are!" (1 John 3:1).

"Praise be to the God and Father of our Lord Jesus Christ! In his great mercy he has given us new birth into a living hope . . . and into an inheritance that can never perish, spoil or fade— kept in heaven for you" (Peter 1:3-4).

Suffering

Biblical Definition:

Greek, *pascho*, to "suffer" in mind or body. Often used in combination with words such as . . . *long* . . . *loss* . . . *need* . . . *shame* . . . *persecution*. The Greek *pascho* is the basis of our English word *passion*—to suffer with great pain or emotion.

Biblical References:

"Praise be to . . . the God of all comfort, who comforts us in all our troubles, so that we can comfort those in any trouble with the comfort we ourselves have received from God" (2 Corinthians 1:3-4).

"I consider that our present sufferings are not worth comparing with the glory that will be revealed in us" (Romans 8:18).

"There was given me a thorn in my flesh . . . to torment me. Three times I pleaded with the Lord to take it away from me. But he said to me, 'My grace is sufficient for you, for my power is made perfect in weakness'" (2 Corinthians 12:7-9).

"Dear friends, do not be surprised at the painful trial you are suffering . . . but rejoice that you participate in the sufferings of Christ, so that you may be overjoyed when his glory is revealed" (1 Peter 4:12-13).

"But if you suffer for doing good and you endure it, this is commendable before God. To this you were called, because Christ suffered for you, leaving you an example, that you should follow in his steps" (1 Peter 2:20-21).

Temptation

Biblical Definition:

Greek, *peirasmos*, a "trial" or "temptation." The biblical term refers both to the trial or testing that we experience that makes us vulnerable to temptation, as well as the temptation itself. Temptation is like a lure that draws us into sin and hooks us on sinful habits.

Biblical References:

"When tempted, no one should say, 'God is tempting me.' For God cannot be tempted by evil, nor does he tempt anyone; but each one is tempted when, by his own evil desire, he is dragged away and enticed" (James 1:13-14).

"No temptation has seized you except what is common to man. And God is faithful; he will not let you be tempted beyond what you can bear. But when you are tempted, he will also provide a way out so you can stand up under it" (1 Corinthians 10:13).

"Brothers, if someone is caught in a sin, you who are spiritual should restore him gently. But watch yourself, or you also may be tempted" (Galatians 6:1).

"Submit yourselves, then, to God. Resist the devil, and he will flee from you" (James 4:7).

"Rather, clothe yourselves with the Lord Jesus Christ, and do not think about how to gratify the desires of the sinful nature" (Romans 13:14).

"You, dear children, are from God and have overcome them, because the one who is in you is greater than the one who is in the world" (1 John 4:4).

Worry

Biblical Definition:

Greek, *merimna,* "worry," "care," or "anxious" thought. Worry is anxiety over circumstances beyond our control. Worry is based on the fear that God is not in control of our lives. It is a self-inflicted panic that is the opposite of confidence in God.

Biblical References:

"Do not worry about your life, what you will eat or drink; or about your body, what you will wear. Is not life more important than food, and the body more important than clothes? Look at the birds of the air . . . your heavenly Father feeds them. Are you not much more valuable than they?" (Matthew 6:25-26).

"Who of you by worrying can add a single hour to his life? . . . O you of little faith? So do not worry. . . . But seek first [God's] kingdom and his righteousness, and all these things will be given you as well" (Matthew 6:27,30-33).

"Rejoice in the Lord always. . . . Do not be anxious about anything, but in everything, by prayer . . . present your requests to God. And the peace of God, which transcends all understanding, will guard your hearts and your minds in Christ Jesus" (Philippians 4:4-7).

"Cast all your anxiety on him because he cares for you. . . . And the God of all grace . . . will himself restore you and make you strong, firm and steadfast. To him be the power for ever and ever. Amen" (1 Peter 5:7,10-11).

NOTES

Chapter One—How to Handle Life's Toughest Problems

1. Jay Adams, *Coping with Counseling Crises* (Grand Rapids: Baker Book House, 1976), p. 21.

2. Ibid., pp. 21-22.

3. Ibid., p. 23.

4. Gary Collins, *How to Be a People Helper* (Santa Ana, CA: Vision House, 1976), p. 25.

Chapter Two—Facing a Crisis with Confidence

1. Jayne Crisp, "Crisis Intervention," in Lisa Barnes Lampman, *Helping a Neighbor in Crisis* (Wheaton, IL: Tyndale House, 1997), pp. 9-16.

2. Ibid., p. 10.

3. Ibid., p. 12.

4. Donna Aguilera and Janice Messick, *Crisis Intervention: Theory and Methodology* (St. Louis: C.V. Mosby Co., 1986), pp. 63-77.

TOTALLY SUFFICIENT

by Ed Hindson and Howard Eyrich

Christians and Christian counselors quickly agree that the Bible's message of salvation has the power to radically change lives. Scripture can lead even the most unlikely people to become children of God. But when it comes to our everyday problems and needs, is the Bible really enough? What about the areas of life that are not addressed specifically in Scripture?

Ultimately, can we say Scripture is sufficient for *every* counseling situation?

More than a dozen professionally trained counselors, medical experts, and pastors who are highly respected in their fields respond to the question that is at the very foundation of the controversy in Christian counseling today. Their answers are enlightening, thought-provoking, and even surprising.

An ideal resource for lay counselors and professionals, and anyone involved in offering counsel and encouragement to family and friends.